THE ARMED FORCES OF THE UNITED KINGDOM

THE ARMED FORCES OF THE UNITED KINGDOM

Edited by CHRIS CHANT

David & Charles
Newton Abbot   London   North Pomfret (Vt)

British Library Cataloguing in Publication Data

The armed forces of the United Kingdom.
    1. Great Britain – Armed Forces – Equipment
    I. Chant, Chris
  623'.0941   UC525.G7

   ISBN 0–7153–8024–9

Printed in Great Britain
by Redwood Burn Limited, Trowbridge & Esher
for David & Charles (Publishers) Limited
Brunel House Newton Abbot Devon

Published in the United States of America
by David & Charles Inc
North Pomfret   Vermont 05053   USA

Contents

Foreword

The volume is divided into three sections. The first details the numbers, organisation and equipment of the British Army and gives full technical specifications of the Army's equipment. The second similarly details the numbers and types of vessels and aircraft operated by the Royal Navy and gives the technical specifications of its ships, torpedoes and missiles. The third details the numbers and types of aircraft operated by the Royal Air Force and, in the technical section, gives details of the aircraft and missiles.

Each technical entry has been designed to provide an easily assimilable, but relatively complete, quantity of data, to allow the reader to assess the capabilities of the weapon, ship or aircraft, together with brief notes intended to elucidate its history, design and variants. Where there are variants, the notes indicate to which of the variants the technical specification applies, unless the variants differ so little that the same basic technical specification is applicable to all.

Although pure logic would dictate that aircraft operated by the Army and Royal Navy should be located in the appropriate sections, it has been felt better and neater to include all aircraft in the section on the RAF. However, the aircraft types and strengths operated by the Army and Royal Navy have been included in their respective sections.

The types of Army weapons and equipment covered in this volume are basically:
- (i) armoured fighting vehicles (main battle tanks, light tanks, armoured cars, scout vehicles, armoured personnel carriers and self-propelled artillery)
- (ii) battlefield support artillery missiles
- (iii) anti-tank/assault missiles
- (iv) portable AA missiles
- (v) artillery (conventional and AA)
- (vi) portable anti-tank weapons
- (vii) mortars
- (viii) machine-guns
- (ix) rifles.

Most of the sub-headings for the various categories of weapon are self-explanatory, but some may need a little additional explanation. For the AFVs, for example:

  (i) *Weights*: Empty refers to the vehicle without fuel, ammunition, crew and other movable equipment, while *Weight*: Loaded refers to the vehicle with all these items

  (ii) *Performance*: vertical obstacle refers to the vehicle's ability to cross a vertical 'step', trench refers to the ability to cross a gap and wading refers to the vehicle's ability to move through water barriers (with and without preparation)

 (iii) *Armament* – a coaxial machine-gun is one aligned to fire along the same axis as the main armament.

For artillery:

  (i) *Barrel length* is normally measured in terms of the number of calibres (bore diameters) long it is.

The types of ships and weapons used by the Royal Navy covered in this volume are basically:

   (i) submarines
  (ii) aircraft-carriers (anti-submarine warfare)
 (iii) anti-submarine cruisers
 (iv) helicopter cruisers
  (v) light cruisers (between 5,000 tons/5,080 tonnes and 10,000 tons/ 10,160 tonnes)
 (vi) destroyers (between 3,000 tons/3,048 tonnes and 5,000 tons/ 5,080 tonnes)
 (vii) frigates (between 1,100 tons/1,118 tonnes and 3,000 tons/ 3,048 tonnes)
(viii) assault ships
 (ix) minehunters/minesweepers
  (x) offshore patrol craft (between 500 tons/508 tonnes and 1,100 tons/ 1,118 tonnes)
 (xi) large patrol craft (between 100 tons/101.6 tonnes and 500 tons/ 508 tonnes)
 (xii) missiles (shipborne surface-to-air, surface-to-surface)
(xiii) torpedoes.

Within each technical entry for ships there are 12 sub-headings:

  (i) *Class* indicates the class of ship to which the vessel belongs, thus allowing the reader to compare the ship with others of the same class used by different nations

  (ii) *Displacement* indicates the 'weight' of the vessel, in four different categories:
    (a) light: actual minimum displacement in seagoing condition
    (b) standard: weight of vessel fully manned and equipped, with stores and ammunition, but without reserve feed-water or fuel (also known as the Washington Treaty tonnage)
    (c) normal
    (d) full load: as (b) but with reserve feed-water and fuel (for submarines, the two usual displacement figures are surfaced and dived tonnages, which are self explanatory)

 (iii) *Dimensions* indicate the overall length, maximum beam and maximum draught of the vessel unless otherwise specified

 (iv) *Armament* indicates the vessel's weapons in five categories:

(a) guns (excluding saluting guns), with the number of weapons in each calibre, and generally their mountings

(b) missiles, with their launchers, functions and reserve rounds

(c) A/S weapons, designed for operations against submarines: these are mostly small-calibre torpedo tubes (sometimes listed under torpedo tubes), depth-charge racks, depth-charge throwers (DCTs), rocket-launchers and various types of pattern-bomb throwers

(d) torpedo tubes, usually for anti-ship work, and listed by calibre and number of tubes in a mounting

(e) aircraft

(v) *Radar and electronics* indicate the types and functions of the radar and other electronic combat aids carried by the ship

(vi) *Sonar* indicates the type of sonar (asdic) carried

(vii) *Powerplant* indicates the type and power of the ship's engines, and the number of shafts driven

(viii) *Speed* indicates the vessel's speed in knots

(ix) *Range* indicates the vessel's range at a given speed or speeds

(x) *Crew* indicates the vessel's complement: where the sign (+) is used, the figure before the sign shows the number of officers carried, that after the sign the number of other ranks carried

(xi) *Used* indicates the countries which use that class of vessel

(xii) *Notes* give further information about alterations, sister-ships, and key dates.

The types of RAF aircraft and weapons covered in this volume are basically the following:

(i) combat aircraft currently in service

(ii) communications/liaison aircraft currently in service

(iii) training aircraft currently in service

(iv) missiles (air-to-air, air-to-surface).

Within each technical entry for aircraft there are 15 sub-headings (16 in the case of helicopters):

(i) *Type* indicates the purpose for which the aircraft is used

(ii) *Crew* indicates the normal operating crew of the aircraft, plus the number of passengers that can be carried (where appropriate)

(iii) *Wings* indicates the structural type and medium of the wings

(iv) *Fuselage* indicates the structural type and medium of the fuselage (body)

(v) *Tail unit* indicates the structural type and medium of the tail unit

(vi) *Landing gear* indicates the nature and operation of the landing gear

(vii) *Powerplant* indicates the type and power of the engine used in the aircraft

(viii) *Fuel capacity* indicates the internal, and where applicable the external, fuel capacity of the aircraft

(ix) *Avionics* indicates the nature of the radar and other electronic operational equipment carried by the aircraft (in general only combat radar and electronics have been identified)

(x) *Armament* indicates the weapons that can be carried internally and externally (the specifications for the more modern aircraft are fuller, because these aircraft can carry a more diverse and potent variety of weapons, especially on their external hardpoints)

(xi) *Dimensions* indicates the overall (except where specified to the contrary) wingspan, length and height of the aircraft

(xii) *Wing area* indicates the gross wing area of the aircraft

(xiii) *Weights* indicates the aircraft's empty equipped, normal take-off and maximum take-off weights

(xiv) *Performance* indicates the aircraft's performance in terms of speed (maximum and cruising), climb, service ceiling and various ranges

(xv) *Used* indicates the user nations

(xvi) *Notes* gives a brief summary of the aircraft's history and variants, where applicable.

The same parameters have been applied to helicopters, *mutatis mutandis*. *Rotor* has replaced *Wings*; *Tail unit* has been omitted (generally being included with *Rotor*); *Dimensions*: span referring to the diameter of the main rotor and length generally referring to the length of the helicopter's fuselage; and *Rotor disc area* replacing *Wing area*, and referring to the area of the main rotor disc(s).

For missiles in every section the categories of sub-heading within each entry are as follows:

(i) *Type* indicates the function of the missile

(ii) *Guidance* indicates the means by which the missile is guided in flight, and the principle used for this purpose

(iii) *Dimensions* indicate the fin span, body diameter and length of the missile

(iv) *Booster* indicates the method by which the missile is accelerated at launch from stationary towards cruising speed

(v) *Sustainer* indicates the method by which the missile is maintained at cruising speed

(vi) *Warhead* indicates the nature and weight of the warhead (occasionally the weight of the explosive within the warhead)

(vii) *Weights* indicates the weight of the missile at launch and after all fuel has been burnt out

(viii) *Performance* indicates the weapon's speed, range and (where relevant) the circular error probable (CEP) or the radius of the circle within which half the missiles fired at the same target may be expected to fall

(ix) *Used* indicates user nations

(x) *Notes* give a brief summary of the missile's history and variants, where applicable.

In each section all measurements are given in Imperial and metric equivalents, the following conversion factors having been used:

pound to kilogram: divide by 2.2046
gallon to litre: multiply by 4.54596 (NB: 1 US gallon equals 0.8327 Imperial gallon, or 3.78542 litres)
inch to centimetre: multiply by 2.54
inch to millimetre: multiply by 25.4
foot to metre: divide by 3.2808
ft^2 to m^2: divide by 10.7639
mile (and mph) to kilometre (and kph): multiply by 1.6093.

The British Armed Forces
Introduction

The United Kingdom of Great Britain and Northern Ireland has a
total population in the order of 55,960,000 and a gross national
product (estimated for 1978) of US $302 billion (£160.362 billion).
Despite her retention of vestigial colonial areas and her position as
titular head of the Commonwealth of former colonies, dominions and
mandated territories, Great Britain has slowly but inevitably withdrawn
from any real pretensions of world power, and today concentrates her
military efforts towards a strengthening of the North Atlantic Treaty
Organisation, of which she was a founder member in 1949.

Although Great Britain still has a few commitments outside Europe
(for example in Belize, Brunei, Hong Kong and Zimbabwe-Rhodesia),
it is against the NATO commitment to Europe that the country's
defence forces must be seen. The founder members of the Organisation
of the North Atlantic Treaty, as NATO should formally be styled,
were the following: Belgium, Canada, Denmark, France (which in
1966 left the integrated military organisation), Great Britain, Iceland,
Italy, Luxembourg, the Netherlands, Norway, Portugal and the United
States. These 12 founder states were joined by Greece (which left the
Defence Planning Body in 1974) and Turkey in 1952, and by the
Federal German Republic (West Germany) in 1955; at the present Spain
is considering whether or not to press her claim for membership of the
alliance.

Despite the general weakness of her economy and the small size of her
armed forces, whose manpower is entirely voluntary, Great Britain
remains an essential component of the NATO alliance. Though it is
generally reckoned that any decisive encounter between the forces of the
North Atlantic Treaty Organisation and of the Warsaw Treaty
Organisation (WTO, otherwise the Warsaw Pact, comprising at its
inception in 1955: Albania, which left the pact in 1968; Bulgaria;
Czechoslovakia; East Germany; Hungary; Poland; Romania; and the Union
of Soviet Socialist Republics) will take place on the North German Plain,
the strategic options open to the USSR and its satellites are wide. Thus
while Great Britain contributes a significant portion of her land and air
forces to the Allied Forces Central Europe (AFCENT), specifically the

Northern Army Group (NORTHAG) responsible for the defence of the region north of the line Göttingen – Liège, she is also one of the few nations to contribute forces to more than one region of the Allied Command Europe (ACE), whose Supreme Headquarters, Allied Powers in Europe (SHAPE) at Casteau near Mons in Belgium controls the European theatre's main forces. Great Britain is the only European member of NATO to contribute forces to each of the triad elements on which NATO's deterrent plans depend; at the same time she is one of only two European NATO states to provide forces for all three major NATO operational commands: ACE, Allied Command Atlantic (ACLANT) and Allied Command Channel (ACCHAN).

Britain's commitment to the northern European theatre is important to the defence of this vital region, but the country's location is also vital for the safe arrival of reinforcements of men and *matériel* from across the Atlantic, for the denial of the North Atlantic to Russian naval and air forces, and as a linchpin between NATO's northern flank (Denmark, Norway, Schleswig-Holstein and the Baltic Approaches) and the central European theatre.

Of the three main commands in NATO, two are always headed by American officers: the Supreme Allied Commander Europe (SACEUR) is the Commander-in-Chief of the United States Forces in Europe, and the Supreme Allied Commander Atlantic (SACLANT), commanding ACE and ACLANT respectively. However, the third major commander is always a British admiral, the Commander-in-Chief Channel (CINCCHAN) at the head of ACCHAN. SACEUR has two deputies, one a British officer and the other a German officer; the Deputy SACLANT is a British admiral; and the commander of the Allied Forces Northern Europe (AFNORTH), designated CINCNORTH, has so far always been a British officer.

Within the NATO alliance, the largest contributor in every respect is the United States of America. The latest year for which fairly accurate figures are available is 1978: in this year the USA spent some 5 per cent of its gross national product (GNP) on defence, an average of US $481 per capita; in terms of GNP, Great Britain comes next with 4.7 per cent, then West Germany with 4.1 per cent, France with 4 per cent, the Netherlands with 3.4 per cent, Belgium and Portugal with 3.3 per cent, and Norway 3.2 per cent; the other NATO members contribute less than 3 per cent of their GNPs to defence. However, in terms of per capita defence expenditure, the USA is followed by West Germany with US $429, France with US $333, Norway with US $313, Belgium with US $312, the Netherlands with US $303, Great Britain with US $252, and Denmark with US $247; the other NATO members contribute considerably smaller per capita quotas.

DEFENCE POLICY

The Defence Estimates 1979, presented to Parliament by the Secretary of State for Defence in February 1979, had the following to say on the associated topics of defence and deterrence: 'Until the Government's objective of general and complete disarmament under strict and effective international control has been met . . . a substantial defence effort remains necessary; and, indeed, is a precondition of successful political action. The balanced modernisation and improvement which the [NATO] Alliance is making to its forces are designed to maintain the credibility of the deterrent strategy of flexible response. This calls for the ability to meet aggression in any form, and at any level in a way appropriate to the level of force used, and to demonstrate to any aggressor that the risks from aggression far outweigh any prospect of gaining an advantage. NATO does not need to match the Warsaw Pact in every category of armament to achieve the flexibility necessary for this ability to deter, but it does need a wide range of forces embracing conventional units, a theatre nuclear capability and strategic nuclear forces. These must be both credible in themselves and sufficiently closely linked together to convince an aggressor that he could overcome one level of capability only at the expense of incurring a response from the next level in a process which would continue, if necessary, up to the strategic level.'

This defence 'posture' is in no way exceptional in its general outline, and would be satisfactory if its basic need, for a credible deterrent made up of balanced and effective conventional and nuclear forces, were met. But this is not the case in the specifically British, and generally western European, defence establishments;

1. Conventional forces are too small, short of training for financial reasons, and generally lacking the backing of sufficient reserve forces and weapons and of adequate supplies of munitions.

2. Despite recent improvements, NATO integration in every respect – from the interchangeability of refuelling hose connections to the command structure – is still sadly lacking, especially in comparison with the high level of integration achieved by the Russian-dominated Warsaw Pact forces.

3. Peacetime procedures and a virtually total refusal to entertain any element of risk mean that the NATO forces are generally deployed in the wrong places and without the transport and command ability to ensure swift large-scale movement to the right places in the event of an eastern bloc offensive launched without warning.

4. Western defence spending is wholly inadequate: at a time when analysts agree that Russia's defence spending averages some 12 per cent of GNP, that of the USA is only 5 per cent; and while the average spending of the other NATO countries on defence is in the order of 3.69 per cent, that of the other Warsaw Pact countries is some 3.55 per cent, reflecting the importance of the two senior partners in each alliance, and the relatively low level of spending by the relatively affluent European NATO countries compared with a relatively high spending by the comparatively poorer eastern European member states of the Warsaw Pact.

5. Despite a continuous history of Russian territorial and political aggrandisement in recent years (Poland, Lithuania, Latvia and Estonia in 1939; Finland in 1939–1940 and 1944; much of eastern Europe in 1944–1945; East Germany in 1953; Hungary in 1956; Czechoslovakia in 1968; and recent Russian support and direct intervention in areas such as the Horn of Africa in 1978–1979 and Afghanistan in 1979–1980), the western alliance appears culpably unwilling even to admit the nature of Russia's long-term aims, let alone prepared to do anything about them other than provide inadequate forces for the defence of their own territories, ignoring the wider implications of Russia's global strategy for the sake of their consumer-oriented economies and politics.

Great Britain must take a fair portion of the blame for these five main failings. The armed forces themselves are fully aware of the problems, but they have been stymied by a succession of governments bent more on short-term political and economic expediency than on long-term realism in both political and military spheres. It is almost as though Great Britain, as one of the dominant European partners in the NATO alliance, has suffered from governments which are convinced, or have convinced themselves, that there exists a latter-day 'ten-year rule', whose actuality cannot publicly be admitted, but whose very existence will in some impossible way allow the government to divine if and when the Soviet Union intends to launch a western European war, and provide the government with just sufficient time to re-arm the country. Given the current strength of the Soviet Union and the Warsaw Pact countries, the hope can only be pious rather than sanguine.

THE MINISTRY OF DEFENCE

The defence of Great Britain, and the institution and control of her various overseas wars, has long been of paramount importance: too important, indeed, to be controlled by a single individual as was the case with most other departments of government. There thus evolved a strangely effective system of multiple control, planning and command involving the sovereign, Parliament, the War Office with its Secretary of State, the Admiralty with its Secretary of State, and from 1918 the Air Ministry with its Secretary of State also. Other interested departments were also involved as necessary, but the growing complexity of national warfare finally persuaded the government that some central agency was needed for the co-ordination of the British Empire's military and naval forces. In 1902, therefore, the Conservative administration set up a temporary Committee of Imperial Defence to advise the prime minister, Arthur Balfour, on matters of imperial defence in the aftermath of the disastrous military conduct of the 2nd Boer War (1899–1902). The Committee of Imperial Defence became permanent in 1904, but its duties were suspended between 1914 and 1919 in favour of specialised committees. Plenary sessions of the Committee of Imperial Defence, whose numbers had by that time risen from 11 to 18, began again in 1922. Although the Committee proved in many ways useful in planning and co-ordination, it was hamstrung by its advisory nature and overextended deliberations, and was again suspended on the outbreak of World War II in September 1939 in favour of the War Cabinet. In 1946 it was decided not to revive the Committee of Imperial Defence.

To replace the Committee of Imperial Defence a two-part structure was established: a cabinet defence committee during 1946, and on 1 January 1947 a Ministry of Defence. Despite its title, the latter exercised no command responsibility, being an administrative and liaison body to co-ordinate the efforts of the government on the one hand and the three service ministries on the other. Although it proved itself a useful body, successive governments and the more far-sighted chiefs realized that the growing complexity of modern military affairs, combined with the 'triphibian' unity of both limited and total warfare, could be better served by a revised Ministry of Defence combining the administrative functions of the current ministry with the command functions of the service ministries. Admiral of the Fleet the Lord Mountbatten of Burma, who had been First Sea Lord between 1955 and 1959 and Chief of the Defence Staff from the summer of 1959, was instrumental in bringing the limitations of the system home to the Conservative administration of the period, and in bringing about the reform of the whole British high command structure instituted by the Secretary of State for Defence, Peter Thorneycroft, from the autumn of 1963. The changes culminated in the formal establishment of a new central Ministry of Defence on 1 April 1964, with Peter Thorneycroft as its first Secretary of State. He was succeeded on 16 October of the same year by Dennis Healey on the coming of the Labour Government.

Under the Secretary of State there is now a unified Ministry of

Defence consisting, in essence, of central staffs concerned with strategy and general defence policy, and of armed forces staffs concerned with with administration and command of the three armed services. The function of the Ministry is to 'ensure effective co-ordination . . . of all questions of policy and administration which concern the fighting Services as the instruments of an effective strategy', with the main elements of the country's overall defence policy decided at cabinet level, with the help of a Committee on Defence and Overseas Policy which replaced the previous Defence Committee of the Cabinet. The key to the whole new structure was the paramount position of the Secretary of State for Defence, the former service ministers being downgraded to the rank of Ministers of State to 'discharge whatever responsibilities the Secretary of State [may] delegate to them from time to time over the whole Defence field. Among their primary functions [is] to execute policy on behalf of the Secretary of State in respect of a designated Service.'

The Ministry of Defence reached perhaps its definitive form in 1969: at its head is the Secretary of State for Defence aided by two parliamentary subordinates, the Minister of Defence for Administration and the Minister of Defence for Equipment. On the next rung down the ministry ladder is a body whose precise function is still unclear, and whose responsibilities are frequently bypassed by the Secretary of State: the Defence Council chaired by the Secretary of State and consisting of the two Ministers of Defence, the Parliamentary Under-Secretaries of State (Royal Navy, Army and Royal Air Force), the Chief of the Defence Staff and the three Chiefs of Staff, the Chief Adviser (Projects and Research), the Chief Adviser (Personnel and Logistics) and the Permanent Under-Secretary of State. However, the functions of the Defence Council are in general only formal, and the chain of command runs for administrative and procurement purposes straight down to the next rung, to the Permanent Under-Secretary of State and his subordinate Second Permanent Under-Secretaries of State (Administration) and (Equipment), and to the Chief Adviser (Projects and Research); and runs for operational purposes straight down to the Chiefs of Staff Committee, made up of the Chief of the Defence Staff and the three Chiefs of Staff. Paralleling the Chiefs of Staff Committee are the Admiralty Board of the Defence Council, the Army Board of the Defence Council and the Air Force Board of the Defence Council, the controlling bodies of the Navy, Army and Air Force Departments which run the three armed services. It should be noted, however, that although in certain respects the three Boards of the Defence Council are equal in status with the Chiefs of Staff Committee, operational control of the armed forces passes from the Chiefs of Staff Committee straight to the Defence Staff consisting of the Central Defence Staff, the Naval Staff, the General Staff and the Air Staff. At the same level as the Defence Staff on the other side of the ladder are the Permanent Under-Secretary of State's Department (eight Deputy Under-Secretaries of State) and the Defence Scientific Staff (two Deputy Chief Advisers) controlling the Central Defence Scientific Staff, and the Chief Scientists (Royal Navy), (Army) and (Royal Air Force).

The three Boards of the Defence Council controlling the services are all constituted in a similar fashion, with the Secretary of State as chairman; the two Ministers of Defence and the relevant Parliamentary Under-Secretary of State as vice-chairmen; and as members the relevant service heads, the vice chief of staff, the relevant Chief Scientist, the relevant Deputy Under-Secretary of State and the two Second Permanent Under-Secretaries of State. Each board is supported by the relevant service's armed force, scientific and political/administrative staffs.

THE BRITISH ARMY

The British Army numbers on 1 April 1980, according to government estimates, some 153,800 men, 6,200 women and 7,500 men enlisted outside Great Britain, this latter including some 6,400 Gurkhas. This total of 167,500 men and women constitutes about 50.79 per cent of the armed forces' total manpower strength of 329,800. Compared with other armies that of Britain is small, but it should be explained that quantity does not in this case reflect quality, and that as a long-standing volunteer force the British Army has many advantages in terms of training and morale. Many armies rely on conscription for their larger manpower strengths, and have less than a year on average to try to turn frequently unwilling conscripts into effective field troops.

The basic unit composition and equipment of the British Army is dealt with in the tabular material prefacing the technical entries' section, and so it is with the formations and the deployment of these formations with which we are here concerned. (All data are generally accurate as at 1 April 1979, and no account is taken of temporary and emergency movements.)

The British Army has two main tasks to fulfil in time of war: the defence of continental Europe in conjunction with other NATO forces, and the defence of the United Kingdom of Great Britain and Northern Ireland. These tasks are reflected in the peacetime stationing of major forces in Germany (the British Army of the Rhine, or BAOR) and in Great Britain (United Kingdom Land Forces, or UKLF), to be supplemented in war by some 124,300 men of the Regular Reserve, and another 55,100 men of the Territorial Army and Volunteer Reserve.

The BAOR consists of I (British) Corps, comprising a corps headquarters, four armoured division headquarters, one artillery division headquarters and the 5th Field Force headquarters, with some 55,000 men under command. The BAOR disposes of the following: 8 armoured regiments, 5 armoured reconnaissance regiments, 15 infantry battalions, 9 field artillery regiments, 1 heavy artillery regiment, 1 missile (Lance) regiment, 1 anti-tank artillery regiment (equipped with Swingfire AT missiles and divided into 4 independent batteries attached to each of the 4 armoured divisions), 2 air defence regiments (equipped with AA missiles and guns), 1 locating regiment, 4 armoured division engineer regiments, 1 amphibious engineer regiment, and 5 regiments of the Army Air Corps. In the event of war I (British) Corps would be reinforced by those units of the 5th Field Force retained in Great Britain, the 7th Field Force, other units currently in Great Britain, reservists, and some elements of the support and training organisation of the British Army: at full strength the BAOR will absorb about 70 per cent of the British Army's front-line strength, and will form, together with Belgian, Dutch and West German forces, the combat element of NORTHAG for the defence of the North German Plain. Also in Germany, but uncommitted to NATO, is the Berlin Field Force of some 3,000 men allocated to garrison duties in the British sector of this four-power city, and comprising three infantry battalions.

The defence of the British Isles is the responsibility of UKLF, which controls all land forces in Great Britain, including those for deployment to the continental theatre in time of war. Currently in Great Britain are three field forces: based in south-east England is the 6th Field Force (3 Regular and 2 TAVR battalions), which together with a Logistic Support Group forms the UK Mobile Force (UKMF); in eastern England is the 7th Field Force (3 Regular and 2 TAVR battalions), earmarked for German deployment in time of war; in the south-west of England is the 8th Field Force (3 Regular and 2 TAVR battalions), for use in the protection of vital national and NATO installations in Great Britain. Other Regular and TAVR units in the country would also be used for this task, as would additional reservists and men of the Army's support and training organisation. Allocated to the ACE Mobile Force (Land) but maintained in Great Britain is one battalion group of about 1,800 men. (ACE Mobile Force is part of SACEUR's Strategic Reserve for deployment in any part of the ACE theatre.) Also held in Great Britain for ready deployment is the bulk of the 22nd Special Air Service Regiment.

The 'troubles' in Northern Ireland have also absorbed a fair proportion of British strength: under the command of Headquarters Northern Ireland are three infantry brigade headquarters: these control 1 armoured reconnaissance regiment, 5 resident infantry battalions, 8 other units in an infantry role, 1 SAS detachment, 3 Army Air Corps squadrons and 1 Army Air Corps flight. There are also 7,750 men available in 11 battalions of the Ulster Defence Regiment.

Units in Great Britain thus comprise 2 armoured regiments, 4 armoured reconnaissance regiments, 31 infantry battalions (including 1 Ghurkha), 4 field artillery regiments, 1 medium artillery regiment, 1 guided-weapon regiment, 1 air defence regiment, 4 engineer regiments, 1 SAS regiment and 1 Army Air Corps Regiment. These Regular Army forces are supported by the following TAVR units: 2 armoured reconnaissance regiments, 38 infantry battalions, 2 field artillery regiments, 3 air defence regiments, 7 engineer regiments, 2 SAS regiments, and 1 regiment of the Honourable Artillery Company.

Other British Army forces are located as follows: in Belize there are 1 armoured reconnaissance troop, 1 infantry battalion, 1 reduced infantry battalion, 1 artillery battery, 1 light air defence troop, 1 reduced engineer squadron and 1 flight of the Army Air Corps; in Brunei is 1 Gurkha infantry battalion; in Canada is a training unit; in Cyprus, attached to the United Nations Forces in Cyprus (UNFICYP), are 1 armoured reconnaissance squadron, 1 infantry battalion minus 2 companies, and 1 flight of the Army Air Corps; also in Cyprus, as garrison of the Sovereign Base Areas, are 1 armoured reconnaissance squadron, 1 infantry battalion plus 2 companies, 1 engineer support squadron, and 1 flight of the Army Air Corps; in Gibraltar are 1 infantry battalion and 1 specialist team of the Royal Engineers; and in Hong Kong, under the command of a field force headquarters, are 3 Gurkha infantry battalions, 1 British infantry battalion, 1 Gurkha engineer field squadron and 1 squadron of the Army Air Corps.

The British Army is generally of high quality and morale, but has suffered somewhat in recent years by lack of adequate pay scales compared with civilian scales for equivalent work, morale-sapping tours of duty in Northern Ireland, and government policies which seem to encourage the development of advanced weapons which are sold to foreign customers before being issued to British units. Recently, however, pay has been much improved, and the pace of introduction of new weapons increased, with a consequent beneficial effect on recruitment and morale. As with the other British armed services, though, pay and conditions must be further enhanced, and greater thought given to the build-up of reserves (both of men and *matériel*) to ensure adequate wartime supplies.

THE ROYAL NAVY

The Royal Navy and Royal Marines number on 1 April 1980, according to government estimates, 70,600 men, 3,800 women and 400 men enlisted outside Great Britain. This total of 74,800 men and women constitutes about 22.68 per cent of the armed forces' total manpower strength of 329,800. Despite the relatively small size of the Royal Navy, it should be emphasised, quality of men and ships is generally high, reflecting the force's volunteer manning and a history of advanced naval technology.

The basic strength and equipment of the Royal Navy is dealt with in the tabular material prefacing the technical entries' section, and so it is with the deployment of these forces with which we are here concerned. (All data are generally accurate as of 1 April 1979, and no account is taken of temporary and emergency movements.)

The Royal Navy deploys the nuclear strategic deterrent force of Great Britain, in the form of the four 'Resolution' class nuclear-powered ballistic missile submarines. These are each fitted with launch tubes for 16 Polaris A-3 submarine-launched missiles, which are currently being upgraded in terms of warhead capability and targeting accuracy. However, the continued credibility of these missiles cannot be sustained for long into the 1980s, and the British government is currently attempting to make up its mind about what to do next. The most logical solution, and the one favoured by the Royal Navy, is the replacement of the Polaris force by a similar number of nuclear-powered boats equipped with the Trident submarine-launched ballistic missile just entering service with the US Navy. The Polaris force, it should be noted, is under the operational control of SACEUR as part of Europe's nuclear deterrent.

Under the control of the Commander-in-Chief Fleet (CINCFLEET), who in time of war is also CINCHAN and Commander-in-Chief Eastern Atlantic (CINCEASTLANT), the Royal Navy has several primary missions: firstly, anti-submarine warfare; secondly, maritime air defence and anti-ship warfare; thirdly, anti-mine warfare in coastal waters; fourthly, the safeguarding of sea routes from Great Britain to continental Europe; and fifthly, the protection of offshore interests such as oil installations and fishing fleets. All major units of the fleet are assigned to NATO responsibilities, leaving only a few small and obsolescent vessels for purely national tasks. In time of war, NATO tasks would inevitably take precedence, with the responsibilities for helping to keep the eastern Atlantic free from Russian surface and sub-surface units paramount, to allow the safe arrival of reinforcements and *matériel* from across the Atlantic. In this role the units come under command of SACLANT in Norfolk, Virginia.

The main problems facing the Royal Navy are an acute shortage of high-calibre manpower, the increasing age of a number of important surface units, the fact that many of the older frigates carry only one small anti-submarine helicopter, delays in the completion of new ships and repairs to current vessels, a general lightness of armament for the anti-shipping role, and and inadequacy of reserve missiles carried on board ships.

Also of grave concern must be the paucity of vessels for mine counter-measures, and the total inadequacy of the Royal Navy's offshore protection forces. As with the larger surface units, new vessels of improved capability are appearing, and this will soon begin to benefit the mine counter-measures force, but the recent plans for the offshore protection force still fall far short of what may be considered a minimum, let alone a desirable strength.

Perhaps the weakest major element of the Royal Navy's surface force is in the ships able to operate fixed-wing aircraft. The two ASW/commando carriers *Hermes* and *Bulwark* can operate such machines, but it will not be until the mid-1980s that the three 'Invincible' class ASW cruisers, able to operate Sea Harrier V/STOL aircraft, come into effective service. This period should mark the beginning of a renaissance for the Royal Navy, with the appearance of more of the latest destroyers and frigates, new mine counter-measures vessels, a new type of diesel-powered conventional submarine, the new Stingray anti-submarine torpedo, the Sea Skua anti-shipping missile and a number of other improvements.

The strength of the Royal Navy is generally located in the North Sea, the English Channel, the eastern Atlantic and the Mediterranean, with a single frigate detached to Belize, a naval party on Diego Garcia in the Indian Ocean, and patrol craft in Hong Kong waters.

The Royal Marines consist of some 7,500 men, with a brigade headquarters controlling four Royal Marine commandos and one Royal Marine Commando Regiment of the Royal Artillery, with combat, logistic and helicopter support provided by the Royal Navy. In the event of hostilities, the brigade headquarters and two commandos will be detached to northern Norway, where specialised equipment is stockpiled. In this area the Royal Marines will operate in conjunction with a similar force found by the Royal Netherlands Marine Corps.

THE ROYAL AIR FORCE

The Royal Air Force numbers on 1 April 1980, according to government estimates, some 82,500 men, 5,000 women and 100 men enlisted outside Great Britain. This total of 86,600 men and women constitutes about 26.56 per cent of the armed forces' total manpower strength of 329,800. The quality of Royal Air Force personnel is very high, and given the introduction of new aircraft types, the Royal Air Force is a formidable combat force, designed for limited operations in support of the British Army and Royal Navy, and for the defence of the air over Great Britain. Air support of the Royal Navy is provided by RAF Strike Command, based in Great Britain, operating over the Channel and Eastern Atlantic Air Defence Regions of ACE, while air support of the Royal Navy in the North Sea is also a part of the Strike Command's responsibility as part of the United Kingdom Air Defence Region. The Central Air Defence Region, over the theatre in which the BAOR operates, is the responsibility of the Royal Air Force's other main operation command, RAF Germany.

The Commander-in-Chief Strike Command is also the holder of the NATO appointment of Commander-in-Chief United Kingdom Air Forces, and apart from his responsibilities for the defence of the UK Air Defence Region also provides air support under the aegis of SACEUR and for CINCHAN and SACLANT in the English Channel and eastern Atlantic. The command is organised in four groups: No 1 Group is the strike element (6 Vulcan B.2 and 2 Buccaneer S.2 squadrons), with support in the form of 1 squadron of strategic reconnaissance Vulcan SR.2s, 1 squadron of photographic reconnaissance Canberra PR.9s, 2 squadrons of flight refuelling Victor K.2s, and a number of other squadrons; No 11 Group is responsible for the air defence of the United Kingdom with 2 squadrons of Lightning and 6 squadrons of Phantom II fighters, 1 squadron of Shackleton AEW.2 airborne early warning aircraft, and the SAM missiles (Bloodhound 2 and Rapier) protecting installations of great importance, as well as the ground radar system (including the Ballistic Missile Early Warning System station at Fylingdales); No 18 Group is concerned with maritime tasks, using 4 squadrons of maritime-reconnaissance Nimrod MR.1s and several helicopter squadrons in the search and rescue role; No 38 Group has the primary tasks of offensive support with 1 Harrier GR.3 and 3 Jaguar squadrons (the Harrier squadron is assigned to the ACE Mobile Force and 1 Jaguar squadron to the UK Mobile Force, all 4 squadrons being part of SACEUR's Strategic Reserve), and of transport with 1 VC10 strategic and 4 Hercules tactical freighter squadrons and 3 helicopter transport squadrons. Within Great Britain, Support Command controls large numbers of training units, many of them with aircraft capable of operational roles, and the RAF's servicing facilities.

The BAOR is supported by the RAF Germany, whose commander-in-chief is also Commander-in-Chief 2nd Allied Tactical Air Force. Air defence is entrusted to 2 squadrons of Phantom FGR.2 fighters, with the offensive capability of the force performed by 2 strike squadrons equipped with Buccaneer S.2s, 5 attack and reconnaissance squadrons equipped with Jaguar GR.1s, 2 close-support squadrons equipped with Harrier GR.3s, and 1 transport squadron with Wessex helicopters (to be supplemented in time of war by another such squadron from Great Britain). Air defence of airfields is entrusted to the RAF Regiment, which deploys 1 Bloodhound 2 and 4 Rapier SAM squadrons.

RAF aircraft detached to other areas are controlled by Strike Command, and such detachments are currently to be found in Belize, Cyprus and Hong Kong.

In some respects the RAF can indeed be considered an up-to-date force of great potential. But many aircraft still in front-line units are approaching the ends of their useful lives, and an urgent re-equipment programme is needed. The RAF currently has a requirement for 220 fighter/ground-attack and 165 air defence Tornado variable-geometry aircraft, with many of these already ordered and due to enter service in 1981. Although the Conservative government of 1979 is pledged to the full implementation of a fighter squadron expansion scheme devised under the Labour administration, the fighter aircraft available (Lightning and Phantom) are approaching obsolescence, and the RAF urgently needs a decision on its next type. Ground-attack and close-support are currently well accommodated with the Jaguar and Harrier, but a decision is urgently needed on further Harrier development and procurement ('big-wing' Harrier GR.5 or McDonnell Douglas AV-8B Advanced Harrier) and the next ground-attack aircraft for the RAF. The ubiquitous Canberra is now obsolete, and a replacement in many of its roles is needed.

List of Abbreviations

AA	anti-aircraft
AAM	air-to-air missile
ADAWS	action data automation and weapons system
AEW	airborne early warning
AFV	armoured fighting vehicle
AP	armour-piercing
APC	(i) armoured personnel carrier (ii) armour-piercing capped
AP-T	armour-piercing tracer
APDS	armour-piercing discarding sabot
APDS-T	armour-piercing discarding sabot tracer
APHE	armour-piercing high explosive
API	armour-piercing incendiary
API-T	armour-piercing incendiary tracer
ASM	air-to-surface missile
A/S	anti-submarine
ASW	anti-submarine warfare
ASWGW	anti-submarine wire-guided weapon
AT	anti-tank
ATGW	anti-tank guided weapon
CAAIS	computer assisted action information system
COGOG	combined gas turbine or gas turbine
COSAG	combined steam turbine and gas turbine
ECM	electronic countermeasures
ESM	electronic support measures
FAL	fusil automatique légère
FPB	fast patrol boat
GPMG	general-purpose machine-gun
HE	high explosive
HEAT	high-explosive anti-tank
HESH	high-explosive squash head
HOT	Haut subsonique Optiquement téléguidé tiré d'un Tube
IFF	identification friend or foe
INAS	inertial navigation and attack system
IW	individual weapon
LAW	light assault weapon
LPD	amphibious transport dock
LRMTS	laser ranger and marked target selector
LSW	light support weapon
MAD	magnetic anomaly detector
MBT	main battle tank
NBC	nuclear, biological and chemical warfare
RAP	rocket-assisted projectile
RCL	recoilless rifle
SAM	surface-to-air missile
SAR	search and rescue
SAS	Special Air Service
SLBM	submarine-launched ballistic missile
SP	self-propelled
SSBN	nuclear ballistic missile submarine
SSM	surface-to-surface missile
SSN	nuclear attack submarine
TOW	tube launched optically tracked wire command
USGW	underwater-to-surface guided weapon
V/STOL	vertical/short take-off and landing
VTOL	vertical take-off and landing
WP	white phosphorus

THE
BRITISH
ARMY

THE BRITISH ARMY

Personnel: (at 1 April 1979) 163,700 men and women, including 7,500 enlisted outside the UK (125,100 Regular and 58,900 Territorial and Army Volunteer Reserve reservists)

Headquarters
   1 corps HQ
   4 armoured divisional HQs
   1 artillery divisional HQ

Armoured units
   10 armoured regiments
     9 armoured reconnaissance regiments

Infantry units
   48 infantry battalions
   5 Gurkha infantry battalions
   2 parachute battalions (infantry)
   1 parachute battalion (parachute)
   1 SAS regiment

Artillery and missile units
   18 artillery regiments
     1 heavy
     1 medium
     12 field
     1 guided weapon
     1 commando
     1 anti-tank

     1 locating
   1 missile regiment with Lance SSM
   3 air defence regiments with Rapier SAM

Engineer units
   9 engineer regiments

Army Air Corps
   6 regiments

Equipment

Armour
   900 Chieftain MBTs
   271 FV101 Scorpion light tanks
   290 FV107 Scimitar AT vehicles
   ? FV102 Striker AT vehicles
   178 FV438 and FV712 AT vehicles
   243 FV601 Saladin armoured cars
   200 FV721 Fox scout cars
   1,429 Ferret scout cars
   2,338 FV432 APCs
   60 FV103 Spartan APCs
   600 FV603 Saracen APCs

Artillery
   16 M110 8-in (203-mm) SP gun/howitzers
   31 M107 175-mm SP guns
   50 M109 155-mm SP howitzers

155 FV433 Abbot 105-mm SP howitzers
? FH70 155-mm howitzers
100 105-mm Light Guns
100 M-1956 105/14 howitzers
? Bofors M-1948 light AA guns
(18 M109A2 155-mm SP howitzers)*
(184 FH70 155-mm howitzers)

Missiles and AT weapons
   Lance SSM
   Milan ATGW
   Swingfire ATGW
   Carl Gustav 84-mm AT launcher
   Wombat 120-mm AT RCL
   Rapier/Blindfire SAM
   Blowpipe SAM
   (TOW ATGW)
   (LAW ATGW)

Aircraft
   20 Lynx
   150 Gazelle
   100 Scout
   20 Sioux
   7 Alouette II

* Equipment within brackets is on order.

FV4201 Chieftain

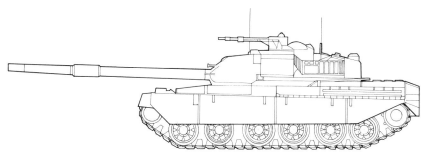

Type: main battle tank
Crew: four
Weights: Empty
      Loaded 121,250 lb (55,000 kg)
Dimensions: Length (gun forward) 35 ft 5 in
      (10.795 m); (hull) 24 ft 8 in
      (7.52 m)
      Width (overall, including
      searchlight) 12 ft (3.66 m)
      Height (overall) 9 ft 6 in (2.895
      m)
Ground pressure: 14.22 lb/in² (0.9 kg/cm²)
Performance: road speed 30 mph (48 kph);
      road range 280 miles (450 km); vertical
      obstacle 3 ft (91.4 cm); trench 10 ft 4 in
      (3.15 m); gradient 60%; ground clearance
      19⅔ in (50.0 cm)
Engine: one 840-bhp Leyland L.60 No 4
      Mark 7A turbo-charged inline multi-fuel
      engine
Armament: one 120-mm L11A2 gun with 53
      rounds of APDS, HESH and Smoke, plus
      one L21A1 (Browning M2) 0.5-in (12.7-
      mm) ranging machine-gun with 300
      rounds, one 0.3-in (7.62-mm) Browning
      machine-gun co-axial with the main arma-
      ment, and one 0.3-in (7.62-mm) Browning
      machine-gun for AA defence on the
      commander's cupola. Some 6,000 rounds
      of 0.3-in (7.62-mm) ammunition are car-
      ried
Armour: 5 9/10 in (150 mm) maximum
Used also by: Iran, Kuwait
Notes: The Chieftain is one of the most
      powerfully armed tanks in the world, and
      also has good protection. Criticism of the
      type, which entered British service in 1967,
      has centred on the tank's weight, lack of

power and general lack of agility. Laser
range-finding is now used, and coupled with
the stabilised gun, this means that targets
can be engaged with a high probability of a
hit at ranges of up to 3,280 yards (3,000
m) with APDS and 8,750 yards (8,000 m)
with HESH ammunition. Night vision and
NBC equipment are standard. There have
been several marks of Chieftain, and other
vehicles have been developed from the
type:

1. Chieftain Mark 1 initial production
model, used only for training
2. Chieftain Mark 2 operational model
with a 650-bhp engine
3. Chieftain Mark 3 with an improved
engine, a new cupola, and a better
auxiliary generator
4. Chieftain Mark 3/G prototype
5. Chieftain Mark 3/2 with better turret
air breathing
6. Chieftain Mark 3/S with yet better
turret air breathing
7. Chieftain Mark 3/3 with an improved
engine, longer-ranged ranging
machine-gun, and a new air cleaning
system

8. Chieftain Mark 4 trials model
9. Chieftain Mark 5 production model
based on the Mark 3/3 with an uprated engine and greater ammunition
capacity
10. Chieftain Mark 6 will be Mark 2s
uprated to Mark 5 standard
11. Chieftain Mark 7 will be Mark 3s and
Mark 3/3s uprated to Mark 5 standard
12. FV4204 Armoured Recovery Vehicle
13. FV4205 Armoured Vehicle-Launched
Bridge.

Alvis FV101 Scorpion

Type: light reconnaissance tank
Crew: three
Weights: Empty
      Loaded 17,548 lb (7,960 kg)
Dimensions: Length 14 ft 5 in (4.39 m)
      Width 7 ft 2 in (2.18 m)
      Height 6 ft 10 in (2.1 m)
Ground pressure: 4.9 lb/in² (0.345 kg/cm²)
Performance: road speed 54 mph (87 kph);
      water speed 4 mph (6.5 kph); range 400
      miles (644 km); verticle obstacle 20 in
      (50.8 cm); trench 6 ft 9 in (2.06 m); gra-
      dient 70%; ground clearance 13¾ in (35.0
      cm); wading 3 ft 6 in (1.07 m) without pre-
      paration
Engine: one 195-bhp Jaguar XK inline petrol
      engine
Armament: one 76-mm gun with 40 rounds
      of HE and HESH, plus one 7.62-mm

machine-gun with 3,000 rounds, co-axial
with the main armament
Armour: classified
Used also by: Belgium, Brunei, Eire,
      Honduras, Iran, Kuwait, Nigeria,
      Philippines, Thailand, United Arab Emirates
Notes: The Scorpion light tank is designed
      specifically for reconnaissance work,
      special attention having been paid to
      making the vehicle as quiet as possible.
      Performance and agility are exceptional for
      a tracked vehicle, and the aluminium
      armour and hard-hitting 76-mm gun will
      enable the type to give a good account of
      itself in combat. Although the range of the
      main armament is 5,470 yards (5,000 m),
      effective range is lower, as the ranging
      method is optical estimating or machine-
      gun ranging. There are several derivatives:

1. Combat Vehicle Reconnaissance
(Tracked) or CVR(T) FV101 Scorpion
light reconnaissance tank, to which
the specification above applies
2. CVR(T) FV102 Striker anti-tank vehicle, with an armament of five BAC
Swingfire AT missile launchers
3. CVR(T) FV103 Spartan armoured personnel carrier, capable of transporting
four infantrymen. The FV103 clearly
does not have the capacity to become
an effective infantry APC, but will
instead be used for the carriage of
special teams
4. CVR(T) FV104 Samaritan armoured
ambulance vehicle, which can carry
four stretchers
5. CVR(T) FV105 Sultan command vehicle with mapboards and a collapsible

penthouse at the rear of the vehicle
6. CVR(T) FV106 Samson armoured recovery vehicle with a winch capable of pulling 12 tons (12,193 kg)
7. CVR(T) FV107 Scimitar anti-reconnaissance vehicle system, armed with a 30-mm Rarden cannon capable of penetrating the armour of reconnaissance vehicles and APCs.

CVR(T) Scimitar

Type: anti-AFV vehicle
Crew: three
Weights: Empty
Loaded 17,196 lb (7,800 kg)
Dimensions: Length 14 ft 5 in (4.39 m)
Width 7 ft 2 in (2.18 m)
Height
Ground pressure: 4.9 lb/in² (0.345 kg/cm²)

Performance: road speed 54 mph (87 kph); water speed 4 mph (6.5 kph); range 400 miles (644 km); vertical obstacle 20 in (50.8 cm); trench 6 ft 9 in (2.057 m); gradient 70%; ground clearance 13¾ in (35.0 cm); the Scimitar is fully amphibious
Engine: one 195-bhp Jaguar XK inline petrol engine
Armament: one 30-mm Rarden cannon with 165 rounds, and one 7.62-mm machine-gun co-axial with the main armament and

provided with 3,000 rounds of ammunition
Armour: classified
Used also by: Belgium
Notes: The Scimitar (FV107) is the last member of the CVR(T) family, and is intended to meet enemy APCs and the like, whose relatively thin armour can be penetrated by the Rarden cannon, which is provided with a range of ammunition including HE, AP, APDS, and Armour Piercing Special Explosive Tracer.

Alvis FV601 Saladin

Type: armoured car
Crew: three
Weights: Empty
Loaded 25,550 lb (11,590 kg)
Dimensions: Length (with gun forward) 17 ft 4 in (5.28 m): (hull) 16 ft 2 in (4.93 m)
Width 8 ft 4 in (2.54 m)
Height 9 ft 7 in (2.93 m)
Ground pressure:
Performance: road speed 45 mph (72 kph); range 250 miles (400 km); vertical obstacle 18 in (46.0 cm); trench 5 ft (1.52 m); gradient 60%
Engine: one 160-bhp Rolls-Royce B.80 Mark 6A inline petrol engine

Armament: one 76-mm gun with 42 rounds of HE, HESH and Smoke, plus one 0.3-in (7.62-mm) machine-gun co-axial with main armament, and one 0.3-in (7.62-mm) AA machine-gun on a pintle mount on the turret roof
Armour: ⅜ in (10 mm) minimum; 1¼ in (32 mm) maximum
Used also by: Bahrain, Indonesia, Kenya, Kuwait, Nigeria, North Yemen, Oman, Qatar, South Yemen, Sri Lanka, Sudan, Tunisia, Uganda, United Arab Emirates
Notes: The Saladin entered British service in 1955, and shares many components with the Saracen. The Saladin has proved well able to cope with mine damage, and its protection, mobility and the punch of its 76-mm HESH round make the type a formidable AFV to this day.

FV721 Fox

Type: armoured car
Crew: three
Weights: Empty
          Loaded 14,079 lb (6,386 kg)
Dimensions: Length (hull) 13 ft 10 in (4.216 m)
          Width 7 ft (2.134 m)
          Height (overall) 7 ft 2½ in (2.2
Ground pressure: 6.5 lb/in² (0.46 kg/cm²)
Performance: road speed 65 mph (104 kph); range 272 miles (438 km); vertical obstacle small; trench 4 ft (1.22 m) with channels; ground clearance 16 in (40.6 cm); wading 30 in (76.0 cm) without preparation
Engine: one 185-bhp Jaguar XK inline petrol engine
Armament: one 30-mm Rarden cannon with 96 rounds, plus one 7.62-mm machine-gun co-axial with the main armament, with 2,600 rounds

Armour:
Used also by: Iran, Nigeria, Saudi Arabia
Notes: The Fox is a reconnaissance vehicle with good performance and a high-powered 30-mm cannon capable of destroying any light AFV at ranges of up to 1,094 yards (1,000 m). To keep weight down, Fox has light alloy armour.

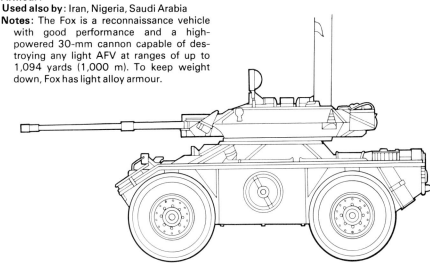

Daimler Ferret

Type: scout car
Crew: two
Weights: Empty
          Loaded 7,680 lb (4,395 kg)
Dimensions: Length 11 ft 1 in (3.385 m)
          Width 6 ft 3 in (1,905 m)
          Height 6 ft 2 in (1.88 m)
Ground pressure:
Performance: road speed 58 mph (93 kph); range 186 miles (300 km); vertical obstacle 1 ft 4 in (40.6 cm); gradient 60%
Engine: one 129-bhp Rolls-Royce B.60 Mark 6A inline petrol engine
Armament: one 0.3-in (7.62-mm) machine-gun
Armour: ⅝ in (16 mm)
Used also by: Burma, Cameroon, Canada, Central African Empire, France, Ghana, Indonesia, Iran, Iraq, Jordan, Kenya, Kuwait, Libya, Malagasy Republic, Malawi, Malaysia, New Zealand, Nigeria, North Yemen, Qatar, Rhodesia, Saudi Arabia, South Africa, South Yemen, Sri Lanka, Sudan, Uganda, United Arab Emirates, Zambia
Notes: The Ferret scout car was introduced into British service in 1953, and has since served in a variety of marks:

1. Mark 1/1 with a Bren or 0.3-in (7.62-mm) machine-gun on a pintle mount in an open top, with 450 rounds
2. Mark 1/2 with a small flat turret armed with a 0.3-in (7.62-mm) machine-gun on top
3. Mark 2/3 is similar to the Mark 1 but with a turret-mounted 0.3-in (7.62-mm) machine-gun and 2,500 rounds. The technical specification above applies to this mark
4. Mark 2/6 is the Mark 2/3 fitted with a BAC Vigilant wire-guided anti-tank missile on each side of the turret. Two spare missiles are carried
5. Mark 3 is a Mark 1/1 with larger wheels, improved suspension and a flotation screen
6. Mark 4 is a Mark 2/3 with larger wheels, improved suspension and a flotation screen
7. Mark 5 or FV712 has larger wheels, improved suspension, a turret of aluminium alloy, and an armament of two BAC Swingfire anti-tank missiles on each side of the turret, which is armed with a 7.62-mm machine-gun. Two spare missiles are carried.

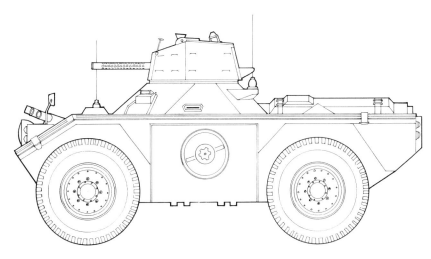

GKN Sankey FV432

Type: armoured personnel carrier
Crew: two, plus up to 10 infantrymen
Weights: Empty 30,290 lb (13,739 kg)
Loaded 33,130 lb (15,280 kg)
Dimensions: Length 17 ft 3 in (5.25 m)
Width 9 ft 2 in (2.8 m)
Height (with machine-gun) 7 ft 6 in (2.286 m); hull) 6 ft 2 in (1.88 m)
Ground pressure: 11.09 lb/in² (0.78 kg/cm²)
Performance: road speed 32 mph (52 kph); water speed 4.1 mph (6.6 kph); range 360 miles (580 km); vertical obstacle 2 ft (60.9 cm); trench 6 ft 9 in (2.05 m); gradient 60%; ground clearance 15¾ in (40.0 cm); wading 3 ft 7½ in (1.1 m) without preparation
Engine: one 240-bhp Rolls-Royce K.60 No 4 Mark 4F inline petrol engine
Armament: one pintle-mounted 7.62-mm GPMG with 2,000 rounds
Armour: ¼ in (6.35 mm) minimum; ½ in (12.7 mm) maximum
Used only by: UK
Notes: The FV432 entered British service in 1963, and is fitted with night-vision equipment and NBC gear as standard. The type has been developed in a number of forms, including:
1. carriage for the Wombat anti-tank weapon and its crew
2. command post
3. fuel and ammunition carrier
4. 81-mm mortar carrier
5. ambulance
6. recovery vehicle with an 8-ton winch
7. artillery observation post
8. carriage for Cymbeline mortar-locating radar
9. Field Artillery Computer Equipment (FACE) carrier
10. minelaying vehicle
11. navigation vehicle
12. 84-mm Carl Gustav carrier
13. No 14 Battlefield Radar carrier
14. APC with a turret-mounted GPMG.

Other vehicles using the same chassis as the FV432 are the Abbot SP gun, the FV434 recovery vehicle, the FV436 with Green Archer mortar-locating radar, and the

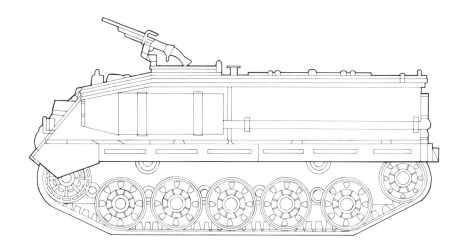

FV438 with Swingfire anti-tank missiles. A versatile vehicle, the FV432 suffers from one major tactical disadvantage: the fact that it has steel rather than aluminium armour means that the vehicle is not inherently buoyant, so flotation screens have to be erected before the vehicle can enter deep water.

CVR(T) Spartan

Type: armoured personnel carrier
Crew: three, plus four infantrymen
Weights: Empty
Loaded 18,015 lb (8,172 kg)
Dimensions: Length 15 ft 10½ in (4.84 m)
Width 7 ft 2 in (2.18 m)
Height 7 ft 4⅜ in (2.25 m)
Ground pressure: about 4.9 lb/in² (0.345 kg/cm²)
Performance: road speed 54 mph (87 kph); water speed 4 mph (6.5 kph); range 400 miles (644 km); vertical obstacle 20 in (50.8 cm); trench 6 ft 9 in (2.06 m); gradient 70%; ground clearance 13¾ in (35.0 cm); the Spartan is fully amphibious
Engine: one 195-bhp Jaguar XK inline petrol engine
Armament: one 7.62-mm (0.3 in) machine-gun with 2,000 rounds of ammunition
Armour: classified
Used also by: Belgium
Notes: The Spartan (FV103) is the APC member of the CVR(T) family whose best known member is the Scorpion (FV101) reconnaissance vehicle.

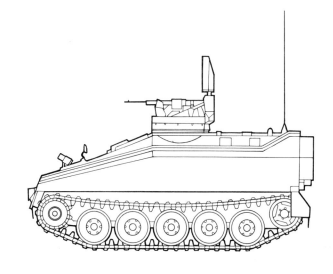

Alvis FV603 Saracen

Type: armoured personnel carrier
Crew: two, plus up to 10 infantrymen
Weights: Empty 17,725 lb (8,040 kg)
Loaded 22,420 lb (10,170 kg)
Dimensions: Length 17 ft 2 in (5.23 m)
Width 8 ft 4 in (2.54 m)
Height 8 ft 1 in (2.46 m)
Ground pressure: 13.93 lb/in² (0.98 kg/cm²)
Performance: road speed 45 mph (72 kph);
range 250 miles (400 km); vertical obsta-
cle 18 in (46.0 cm); trench 5 ft (1.52 m);
gradient 42%
Engine: one 160-hp Rolls-Royce B.80 Mark
6A inline petrol engine
Armament: one 0.3-in (7.62-mm) machine-
gun in the turret with 3,000 rounds, plus
the machine-gun of the infantry squad carried
Armour: $\frac{1}{3}$ in (8 mm) minimum; $\frac{7}{10}$ in (18 mm)
maximum
Used also by: Indonesia, Jordan, Kuwait,
Lebanon, Libya, Nigeria, Qatar, South
Africa, Sudan, Uganda, United Arab Emirates
Notes: The Saracen entered British service in
1953, and has since proved an excellent
vehicle, especially on internal security operations, as a result of its versatility, rug-
gedness, speed, relative quietness and
good cross-country performance.

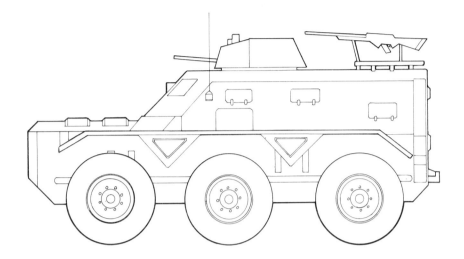

M110

Type: self-propelled howitzer
Crew: 13
Weights: Empty
Loaded 58,000 lb (26,309 kg)
Dimensions: Length 24 ft 6½ in (7.48 m)
Width 10 ft 3½ in (3.14 m)
Height (firing) 21 ft (6.4 m)
Ground pressure:
Performance: road speed 33.5 mph (54 kph);
range 450 miles (724 km); vertical obsta-
cle 40 in (1.016 m); trench 7 ft 9 in (2.362
m); gradient 60%; wading 42 in (1.066 m)
Engine: one 405-hp Detroit Diesel Model
8V71T turbo-charged inline diesel engine
Armament: one 8-in (203-mm) M2A1E1
howitzer with separate loading HE and
Nuclear ammunition
Armour: $\frac{5}{8}$ in (20 mm) maximum
Used also by: Belgium, Greece, Iran, Israel,
Jordan, Netherlands, South Korea, Spain,
USA, West Germany
Notes: The M110 was introduced in 1962,
and is a useful weapon system. The
howitzer fires to a maximum range of
18,375 yards (16,800 m) at a muzzle velocity of 1,950 ft (594 m) per second. The
barrel elevates from +2° to +65°, and total
traverse is 30°. The M110 is in the process
of being supplemented by the M110E2,
which has the new XM201 barrel, which is
8 ft (2.44 m) longer than the M2A1E1, and
can deliver its M106 HE shell to a range of
22,965 yards (21,000 m). The howitzer
will also have a new ammunition, including
rocket-assisted projectiles, incendiary
rounds, HE and nuclear. The weight of the
M110E2, which will enter service as the
M110A1, is 62,100 lb (28,168 kg). The
M110A2 will be the M110A1 fitted with a
muzzle brake.

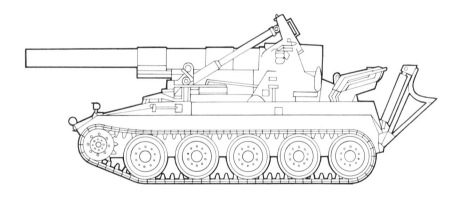

M107

Type: self-propelled gun
Crew: 13
Weights: Empty
     Loaded 62,095 lb (28,166 kg)
Dimensions: Length 37 ft 1 in (11.3 m)
     Width 10 ft 2½ in (3.14 m)
     Height 11 ft 4½ in (3.47 m)
Ground pressure: 13.5 lb/in² (0.95 kg/cm²)
Performance: road speed 33.5 mph (54 kph); range 450 miles (724 km); vertical obstacle 40 in (1.016 m); trench 7 ft 9 in (2.362 m); gradient 60%; wading 42 in (1.066 m)
Engine: one 405-hp Detroit Diesel Model 8V71T turbo-charged inline diesel engine
Armament: one 175-mm L/60 gun with separate loading HE ammunition
Armour: ⅘ in (20 mm) maximum
Used also by: Greece, Iran, Israel, Italy, Netherlands, South Korea, Spain, USA, Vietnam, West Germany
Notes: The M107 uses the same chassis as the M110, and is in the process of being phased out in favour of the dual-purpose M110A1 and M110A2 self-propelled howitzers. The M107 fires its 147-lb (66.6-kg) shell at a muzzle velocity of 3,028 ft (923 m) per second to a range of 35,750 yards (32,700 m). Elevation is from +2° to +65°, and traverse is 30° left and right. Five of the crew are carried on the M107, and the other eight on the accompanying M548. The M107 entered service in 1962–3.

M109

Type: self-propelled howitzer
Crew: six
Weights: Empty
     Loaded 52,460 lb (23,796 kg)
Dimensions: Length 20 ft (6.09 m)
     Width 10 ft 3½ in (3.14 m)
     Height 10 ft (3.04 m)
Ground pressure: 11.4 lb/in² (0.8 kg/cm²)
Performance: road speed 34 mph (55 kph); range 75 miles (120 km); vertical obstacle 21 in (53.3 cm); trench 6 ft (1.83 m); gradient 60%; wading 5 ft (1.524 m)
Engine: one 405-hp Detroit Diesel Model 8V71T turbo-charged inline diesel engine
Armament: one 155-mm L/23 howitzer with 28 rounds of Canister, Chemical, HE or Nuclear ammunition, plus one 0.5-in (12.7-mm) Browning M2 AA machine-gun with 500 rounds
Armour: 1½ in (38 mm) maximum
Used also by: Austria, Belgium, Canada, Denmark, Iran, Israel, Italy, Libya, Netherlands, Norway, Spain, Switzerland, USA, West Germany
Notes: The M109 self-propelled howitzer entered service in 1961, and in most respects other than gun calibre is identical with the M108. The 155-mm howitzer is capable of a rate of fire of 45 rounds per hour, and fires its 95-lb (43-kg) shell to a range of 15,975 yards (14,608 m). The turret has a traverse of 360°. The M109A1 has an improved howitzer, with barrel length increased from 12 ft 1⅜ in (3.7 m) to 20 ft (6.1 m), and weight to 53,060 lb (24,068 kg). Maximum range of the longer barrel is 19,685 yards (18,000 m). All M109s are to be brought up to M109A1 standard.

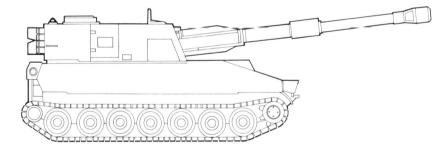

Vickers FV433 Abbot

Type: self-propelled gun
Crew: four
Weights: Empty
Loaded 38,640 lb (17,527 kg)
Dimensions: Length (overall) 19 ft 2 in (5.84 m)
Width 8 ft 8 in (2.64 m)
Height 8 ft 2 in (2.49 m)
Ground pressure: 12.65 lb/in² (0.89 kg/cm²)
Performance: road speed 30 mph (48 kph); water speed 3.1 mph (5 kph); range 242 miles (390 km); vertical obstacle 2 ft (60.9 cm); trench 6 ft 9 in (2.06 m); gradient 60%; wading 3 ft 11¼ in (1.2 m)
Engine: one 213-bhp Rolls-Royce K.60 Mark 4G inline multi-fuel turbo-charged engine
Armament: one 105-mm gun with 40 rounds of HE and HESH, and one 7.62-mm GPMG with 1,200 rounds
Armour: ¼ in (6.35 mm) minimum; ½ in (12.7 mm) maximum
Used also by: India (Value Engineered Abbot)
Notes: Introduced into service with the British Army in 1964, the FV433 Abbot 105-mm SP gun is a highly efficient and mobile weapon system. The range of the gun is some 18,600 yards (17 km), and the barrel life of the piece is at least 10,000 rounds. Although calibre is somewhat small for an SP gun, the Abbot is an effective system because of its mobility, high rate of fire, and lethal ammunition. Vickers have also produced the Value Engineered Abbot by eliminating some of the more sophisticated equipment.

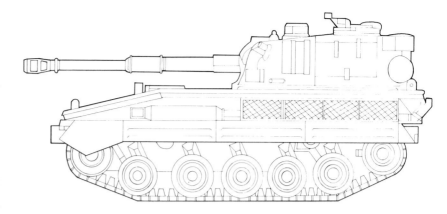

FH70 howitzer

Type: field howitzer
Calibre: 155 mm
Barrel length: 39 cal
Muzzle velocity: 2,713 ft (827 m) per second
Ranges: Maximum 26,250 yards (24,003 m) with normal ammunition; 32,808 yards (30,000 m) plus with extended range ammunition
Minimum
Elevation: −5° to +70°
Traverse: 56° total
Rate of fire: six rounds per minute
Weights: For travel 20,723 lb (9,400 kg)
In firing position 19,400 lb (8,800 kg)
Dimensions: Length 31 ft (9.45 m)
Width
Height 8 ft 4¾ in (2.56 m)

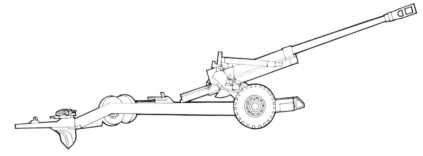

Ammunition: AT, HE, Illuminating and Smoke
Crew: eight to ten
Used also by: Italy, West Germany
Notes: The FH70 is a collaborative venture by the three user countries, design being the responsibility primarily of the UK and West Germany. The piece is provided with an auxiliary power unit capable of providing the gun with a 12.43-mile (20-km) independent travel capability. The HE projectile weighs 96.12 lb (43.6 m).

105-mm Light Gun

Type: light field gun
Calibre: 105 mm
Barrel length: 30.2 cal
Muzzle velocity: 2,325 ft (709 m) per second
Ranges: Maximum 19,140 yards (17,501 m)
Minimum 2,735 yards (2,501 m)
Elevation: −5° to +70°
Traverse: 11° total (360° platform)
Rate of fire: three rounds per minute (sustained); six rounds per minute (maximum)
Weights: For travel 3,900 lb (1,769 kg)
In firing position as above
Dimensions: Length 28 ft 10¼ in (8.8 m) with gun forward; 13 ft 4⅔ in (4.08 m) folded
Width 5 ft 10 in (1.78 m)
Height 7 ft (2.13 m) with gun forward; 4 ft (1.23 m) folded
Ammunition: Anti-Personnel (Canister), HE; HEAT, Illuminating, Smoke, Target Marking and WP
Crew: six
Used also by: some Middle Eastern countries
Notes: The 105-mm Light Gun has been designed as an all-purpose weapon for all climates, its low silhouette, light weight and fast traverse making it a useful anti-tank weapon. Shell weight is 33 lb (15 kg).

M-1956 105/14 howitzer

Type: pack howitzer
Calibre: 105 mm
Barrel length: 16.34 cal including muzzle brake
Muzzle velocity:
Ranges: Maximum 11,565 yards (10,575 m), or 14,217 yards (13,000 m) with RAP
Minimum
Elevation: −5° to +65°
Traverse: 36° total (56° total in AT role)
Rate of fire: eight rounds per minute
Weights: For travel 2,844 lb (1,290 kg)
In firing position
Dimensions: Length 11 ft 11¾ in (3.65 m)
Width 4 ft 11 in (1.5 m)
Height 6 ft 5 in (1.96 m)
Ammunition: AP, HE, HEAT, Illuminating, Smoke and Target Indicating
Crew: six
Used also by: Argentina, Australia, Belgium, Canada, Chile, France, India, Iraq, Italy, Malaysia, New Zealand, Nigeria, Pakistan, Peru, Philippines, Rhodesia, Saudi Arabia, Spain, United Arab Emirates, West Germany, Zambia
Notes: The OTO Melara M-1956 105/14 pack howitzer has been one of the most successful pieces of ordnance produced since World War II. The shell weighs 32.85 lb (14.9 kg), and the penetration of the HEAT round is 4.57 in (116 mm). For AT use, the gun is lowered on its carriage to reduce the silhouette. The whole piece breaks down into 11 loads, the heaviest weighing 269 lb (122 kg).

Bofors M-1948 gun

Type: light anti-aircraft gun
Calibre: 40 mm
Barrel length: 70 cal
Muzzle velocity: 3,280 ft (1,000 m) per second with HE
Ranges: Maximum (horizontal) 4,374 yards (4,000 m); (vertical) 9,842 ft (3,000 m)
Minimum
Elevation: −5° to +90°
Traverse: 360°
Rate of fire: 240 rounds per minute (cyclic)
Weights: For travel 11,354 lb (5,150 kg)
In firing position 10,582 lb (4,800 kg)
Dimensions: Length 20 ft 6¾ in (6.27 m)
Width 7 ft 4½ in (2.25 m)
Height 7 ft 8½ in (2.35 m)
Ammunition: AP-T, APDS-T and HE
Crew: six
Used also by: Austria, Belgium, Denmark, France, Greece, India, Israel, Italy, Netherlands, Norway, Portugal, Spain, Sweden, Turkey
Notes: The M-1948 Bofors AA gun was developed from the prewar M-1936 40-mm gun, and entered service in 1951. Ammunition weight is 2.12 lb (0.96 kg) per round, and the carriage holds 48 rounds, 16 of them above the breech for ready use. There are four models: the M-1948 basic model, the M-1948D with provision for radar control, the M-1948R with provision for radar control, and the M-1948C. Some of the carriages have provision for an auxiliary power unit for limited independent travel.

Carl Gustav M2-550 launcher

Type: man-portable anti-tank rocket launcher
Calibre: 84 mm
Barrel length:
Muzzle velocity: 951 ft (290 m) per second with HEAT
Ranges: Maximum effective 766 yards (700 m)
     Minimum
Elevation:
Traverse:
Rate of fire:
Weights: For travel 33 lb (15 kg)
     In firing position 39.7 lb (18 kg)
Dimensions: Length 3 ft 8½ in (1.13 m)
     Width
     Height
Ammunition: HE and HEAT
Crew: two
Used also by: Eire, Japan, Kenya, Netherlands, Norway, Sweden
Notes: The Carl Gustav M2-550 is an improved version of the Carl Gustav M2 in service with the armies of Austria, Canada, Denmark, Eire, Ghana, Netherlands, Norway, Sweden, United Arab Emirates, UK, West Germany. The M2-550 has

improved sighting arrangements and a better AT round. This weighs 6.6 lb (3 kg), of which 4.85 is the shell. This can penetrate 15¾ in (400 mm) of armour, but at longer range than the 492 yards (450 m) of the M2's HEAT shell.

Wombat L6 recoilless rifle

Type: anti-tank recoilless rifle
Calibre: 120 mm
Barrel length: 33.33 cal
Muzzle velocity: 1,515 ft (462 m) per second
Ranges: Maximum 1,094 yards (1,000 m) against a static target; 820 yards (750 m) against a moving target
     Minimum
Elevation:
Traverse: 360°
Rate of fire: four rounds per minute
Weights: For travel (portee version) 650 lb (295 kg)
     In firing position as above
Dimensions: Length 12 ft 8 in (3.86 m)
     Width 2 ft 10 in (0.86 m)
     Height 3 ft 7 in (1.09 m)
Ammunition: HESH
Crew: three
Used also by: Australia
Notes: The Wombat was developed as a light successor to the Mobat, and entered British service during the 1960s. Spotting is by a 0.5-in (12.7-mm) rifle. Weight of the whole round is 60 lb (27.2 kg), and of the projectile 28.3 lb (12.84 kg). No details of armour penetration are available, but the round will probably penetrate more than 15¾ in (400 mm) of armour.

Mobat L4 recoilless rifle

Type: anti-tank recoilless rifle
Calibre: 120 mm
Barrel length: 33.33 cal
Muzzle velocity: 1,515 ft (462 m) per second
Ranges: Maximum 875 yards (800 m)
          Minimum
Elevation:
Traverse: 360°
Rate of fire:
Weights: For travel 1,685 lb (764 kg)
        In firing position as above
Dimensions: Length 11 ft 3¾ in (3.45 m)
          Width 5 ft (1.525 m)
          Height 3 ft 10¾ in (1.19 m)
Ammunition: HESH
Crew: three
Used only by: UK
Notes: The Mobat is the Wombat's predecessor, and has much the same performance, as it uses exactly the same round. However, weight is considerably greater than that of the Wombat, and tactical mobility considerably less. Spotting is by a modified 7.62-mm Bren gun attached to the Mobat barrel.

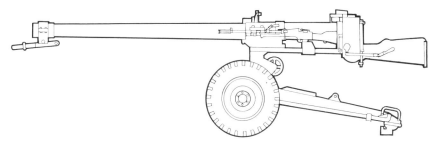

British Aerospace Rapier

Type: land-mobile, air-transportable surface-to-air tactical guided missile
Guidance: semi-automatic command to line-of-sight
Dimensions: Span 15 in (38.1 cm)
          Body diameter 5¼ in (13.3 cm)
          Length 7 ft 4 in (2.24 m)
Booster: IMI Troy dual-thrust solid-propellant rocket
Sustainer: see above

Warhead: 1.1 lb (0.5 kg) SAP high explosive
Weights: Launch 94 lb (42.6 kg)
        Burnt out
Performance: speed probably about Mach 2; ceiling about 16,400 ft (5,000 m); range 530 yards (485 m) to 4½ miles (7.25 km)
Used also by: Australia, Iran, United Arab Emirates, Zambia
Notes: Designed as a battlefield defence system against supersonic aircraft, the Rapier has proved remarkably accurate, to the extent that it is at present fitted only

with an impact fuse. The operator acquires the target visually on receipt of basic data from a surveillance radar, and thereafter keeps his sights on the target. A television camera then follows flares on the tail of the fired missile, and the launcher's computer reduces the missile's deviation from the operator's line-of-sight to nought.

British Aerospace Swingfire

Type: anti-tank guided missile, container-launched from vehicles or from the ground
Guidance: command to line-of-sight by means of wire
Dimensions: Span 1 ft 3$\frac{1}{3}$ in (39.0 cm)
Body diameter 6$\frac{7}{10}$ in (17.0 cm)

Length 3 ft 6$\frac{1}{10}$ in (1.07 m)
Booster: IMI dual-thrust solid-propellant rocket
Sustainer: see above
Warhead: 15.4-lb (7-kg) hollow-charge high explosive
Weights: Launch 59$\frac{1}{2}$ lb (27 kg)
Performance: range 164–4,374 yards

(150–4,000 m); speed 415 mph (667 kph)
Used also by: Belgium, Egypt
Notes: Very powerful weapon. Introduced in 1969. The Swingfire can be launched from a number of vehicle types or by infantry.

Hughes BGM-71A TOW (M151E2)

Type: heavy anti-tank missile, tube-launched from a vehicle or the ground
Guidance: automatic command to line-of-sight by means of wire
Dimensions: Span 13$\frac{1}{2}$ in (34.3 cm)
Body diameter 6 in (15.2 cm)
Length 3 ft 9$\frac{3}{4}$ in (1.162 m)
Booster: Hercules K41 solid-propellant charge
Sustainer: solid-propellant rocket
Warhead: 5.3-lb (2.4-kg) shaped-charge high explosive
Weights: Launch 46.1 lb (20.9 kg)
Burnt out
Performance: range 71–4,100 yards (65–3,750 m); speed 250 mph (402 kph) at maximum range
Used also by: Canada, Denmark, Greece, Iran, Israel, Italy, Jordan, Kuwait, Lebanon, Luxembourg, Morocco, Netherlands, Norway, Oman, Pakistan, Portugal, Sweden, Taiwan, Turkey, Saudi Arabia, South Korea, Spain, USA, West Germany, Yugoslavia
Notes: Very powerful anti-tank weapon system introduced in 1972. TOW = Tube-launched Optically-tracked Wire-command link guided missile.

Messerschmitt-Bölkow-Blohm/ Aérospatiale *Milan*

Type: anti-tank missile, man-portable and tube-launched
Guidance: semi-automatic command to line-of-sight by means of wires
Dimensions: Span 10⅗ in (27.0 cm)
Body diameter 4⅗ in (11.7 cm)
Length 2 ft 6⅓ in (77.0 cm)
Booster: solid-propellant ejector in launch tube
Sustainer: SNPE Artus two-stage solid-propellant rocket
Warhead: 6.6-lb (3-kg) hollow-charge high explosive, capable of penetrating 13.86 in (352 mm) of NATO armour plate at 65°
Weights: Launch 50.8 lb (23.05 kg) for missile and launch/guidance unit
Burnt out
Performance: range 27 yards to 2,187 yards (25–2,000 m); speed 447 mph (720 kph)
Used also by: Belgium, Egypt, France, Greece, Somali Republic, South Africa, Spain, Syria, Turkey, West Germany
Notes: Developed jointly by France and West Germany, the *Milan* (*Missile d'Infanterie Léger Antichar* or infantry light anti-tank missile) is a 2nd-generation AT missile.

After the missile is ejected from the tube, its wings spring open, and the missile is then gathered automatically onto the user's line-of-sight, which remains on the target.

Short Brothers Blowpipe

Type: man-portable surface-to-air tactical guided missile
Guidance: radio command with optical tracking
Dimensions: Span 10⅘ in (27.4 cm)
Body diameter 3 in (7.62 cm)
Length 4 ft 7 in (1.4 m)
Booster: solid-propellant charge
Sustainer: solid-propellant rocket
Warhead: 4.85-lb (2.2-kg) shaped-charge HE
Weights: Launch 24½ lb (11.0 kg)
Burnt out
Performance: speed Mach 1.5; range 2+ miles (3.2+ km)
Used also by: Canada
Notes: Capable of one-man operation, the Blowpipe is designed for close-range battlefield defence against low-flying aircraft and battlefield/assault helicopters. Once he has acquired the target visually, the operator has merely to aim along the sight, fire, and control the flight of the missile by means of a thumb control. The launcher is then discarded, the aiming/control unit then being attached to a fresh round. IFF facility is available with the aiming unit.

Vought MGM-52C Lance

Type: surface-to-surface tactical guided missile, vehicle-launched
Guidance: inertial
Dimensions: Span
Body diameter 22 in (56.0 cm)
Length 20 ft 3 in (6.17 m)
Booster: Rocketdyne P8E–9 liquid-propellant two-part rocket
Sustainer: see above
Warhead: M234 nuclear (10-kiloton) or XM251 HE cluster
Weights: Launch between 3,373 and 3,920 lb (1,530 and 1,778 kg)
Burnt out
Performance: speed Mach 3; range 75 miles (120 km)

Used also by: Belgium, Israel, Italy, Netherlands, USA, West Germany
Notes: The Lance entered service in 1972. Highly mobile, the missile requires a launch crew of eight, and only two vehicles of the M113 family. The Lance can also be delivered to forward sites by aircraft and helicopter.

L1A1 mortar

Type: light mortar
Calibre: 81 mm
Barrel length: 15.68 cal
Muzzle velocity:
Ranges: Maximum 4,920 yards (4,500 m) with standard charge; 6,190 yards (5,660 m) with special charge Minimum 220 yards (201 m)
Elevation: 45° to 80°
Traverse: 360° (10° at 45° elevation)
Rate of fire: 15 rounds per minute
Weights: For travel 89.6 lb (40.62 kg) In firing position 79 lb (35.9 kg)
Dimensions: Length
         Width
         Height
Ammunition: HE, Illuminating, Marking and Smoke WP
Crew: three
Used also by: Canada, Guyana, India, Kenya, Malaysia, New Zealand, Nigeria, South Yemen, United Arab Emirates
Notes: The L1A1 mortar was designed jointly by Canada and the UK. The HE bomb weighs 9.7 lb (4.4 kg). The mortar is also used in the FV 432 mortar carrier.

51-mm mortar

Type: light mortar
Calibre: 51.25 mm
Barrel length: 10.05 cal
Muzzle velocity: 350 ft (107 m) per second
Ranges: Maximum 875 yards (800 m) Minimum 165 yards (150 m)
Elevation:
Traverse:

Rate of fire:
Weights: For travel In firing position 10 lb (4.6 kg)
Dimensions: Length
         Width
         Height
Ammunition: HE, Illuminating and Smoke
Crew: one

Used only by: UK
Notes: The 51-mm mortar is a weapon of great simplicity, but nevertheless effective for short-range engagements. It is designed for infantry use, and the HE bomb weighs 1.75 lb (0.79 kg).

L7 machine-gun

Type: general-purpose machine-gun
Calibre: 7.62 mm
System of operation: gas
Muzzle velocity: 2,750 ft (838 m) per second
Range:
Rate of fire: 750 to 1,000 rounds per minute (cyclic); 100 rounds per minute (rapid fire as LMG); 200 rounds per minute (rapid fire as a sustained-fire weapon)
Cooling system: air
Feed system: metal-link belt
Dimensions: Barrel length 21.54 in (547 mm) without flash hider
         Overall length 48.5 in (1.232 m) as a light machine-gun; 41.25 in (1.048 m) as a sustained-fire machine-gun
         Width
         Height
Weights: 24 lb (10.9 kg) as a light machine-gun; 54 lb (24.51 kg) with L4A1 tripod
Sights: blade (fore) and aperture (rear)
Ammunition: 7.62 mm × 51
Used only by: UK
Notes: The L7 is basically the British version of the Belgian FN MAG. The L7A1 initial

model entered service in 1961, and the modified L7A2 shortly after this. None of the changes was of a major nature.

Light Support Weapon

Type: light support weapon (light machine-gun)
Calibre: 4.85 mm
System of operation: gas
Muzzle velocity: 3,050 ft (930 m) per second
Range:
Rate of fire: 700 to 850 rounds per minute (cyclic)
Cooling system: air
Feed system: 20- or 30-round box
Dimensions: Barrel length 25.4 in (646 mm)
Overall length 35.4 in (900 mm)
Width
Height
Weights: 10.32 lb (4.68 kg) unloaded; 11.6 lb (5.26 kg) loaded
Sights:

Ammunition: 4.85 mm Ball
Used by: under development for trials purposes
Notes: The Light Support Weapon has been produced as the British contender for a NATO competition to find a new calibre and weapon to replace current light machine-guns in the 1980s, and has about 80% commonality of parts with the Individual Weapon produced for the same purpose. The LSW is about 2.2 lb (1 kg) heavier than the IW, is longer and has a higher muzzle velocity. The weapon has a straight-through design, and can be fired from the shoulder as well as from its bipod. However, it seems unlikely that the 4.85-mm round will find NATO favour against the established 5.56-mm rounds, and so production of this interesting weapon is unlikely.

L2A3 Sterling sub-machine gun

Type: sub-machine gun
Calibre: 9 mm
System of operation: blowback
Muzzle velocity: 1,280 ft (390 m) per second
Range: effective 219 yards (200 m)
Rate of fire: 550 rounds per minute (cyclic); 102 rounds per minute (automatic)
Cooling system: air
Feed system: 34-round box
Dimensions: Barrel length 7.8 in (198 mm)
Overall length 27.95 in (710 mm) with stock extended; 19 in (483 mm) with stock folded
Width
Height
Weights: 6 lb (2.72 kg) unloaded; 7.65 lb (3.47 kg) loaded
Sights: blade (fore) and flip, aperture (rear)
Ammunition: 9 mm × 19 Parabellum
Used also by: Ghana, India, Libya, Malaysia, Nigeria, Tunisia and 72 other nations
Notes: The Sterling sub-machine gun is the successor to the Sten gun, and was designed initially in 1942, entering production in 1944. The type in service today is the L2A3, which is sold commercially as the Sterling Mark 4.

L34A1 Sterling sub-machine gun

Type: silenced sub-machine gun
Calibre: 9 mm
System of operation: blowback
Muzzle velocity: 960 to 1,017 ft (293 to 310 m) per second
Range: effective 164 yards (150 m)
Rate of fire: 515 to 565 rounds per minute (cyclic); 102 rounds per minute (automatic); 45 rounds per minute (single shot)
Cooling system: air
Feed system: 34-round box
Dimensions: Barrel length 7.8 in (198 mm)
Overall length 34 in (864 mm) with stock extended; 26 in (660 mm) with stock folded
Width
Height
Weights: 7.94 lb (3.6 kg) unloaded; 9.5 lb (4.31 kg) loaded
Sights: blade (fore) and flip, aperture (rear)
Ammunition: 9 mm × 19 Parabellum
Used only by: UK
Notes: The L34A1 is the silenced version of the L2A3, and is sold commercially as the Patchett/Sterling Mark 5. The silencing

works by allowing much of the propellant gas to escape through the barrel wall through 72 radial holes and move through a diffuser before returning to the barrel to escape through a spiral diffuser extending forward of the muzzle.

Lee-Enfield SMLE No 4 rifle

Type: bolt-action rifle
Calibre: 0.303 in (7.7 mm)
System of operation: manually operated bolt
Muzzle velocity: 2,465 ft (751 m) per second
Range: effective 547 yards (500 m)
Rate of fire: 20 rounds per minute
Cooling system: air
Feed system: 10-round box
Dimensions: Barrel length 25.2 in (640 mm)
          Overall length 44.43 in (1.129 m)
          Width
          Height
Weights: 9.125 lb (4.14 kg) loaded
Sights: protected blade (fore) and adjustable aperture (rear)
Ammunition: 0.303 in Ball Mark VII
Used by: still widely used in former British territories
Notes: The Rifle No 4 Mark 2 was the last production variant of the celebrated SMLE series, and was developed during the late 1920s and early 1930s as successor to the No 1 Mark III. Rugged and accurate, the weapon is capable of a high rate of fire by bolt-action standards, and is still a moderately effective weapon.

L1A1 rifle

Type: self-loading rifle
Calibre: 7.62 mm
System of operation: gas
Muzzle velocity: 2,750 ft (838 m) per second
Range: effective 656 yards (600 m)
Rate of fire: 40 rounds per minute
Cooling system: air
Feed system: 20-round box
Dimensions: Barrel length 21.8 in (554 mm)
          Overall length 45 in (1.143 m)
          Width
          Height
Weights: 9.5 lb (4.3 kg) empty; 11 lb (5 kg) loaded
Sights: trilux (fore) and aperture (rear)
Ammunition: 7.62 mm × 51
Used only by: UK
Notes: The L7 is the FN FAL weapon built under licence, with modifications, in the UK. The most important difference is that the British weapon is capable of firing only single shots, whereas the Belgian weapon is capable of selective fire.

L42A1 rifle

Type: sniper's rifle
Calibre: 7.62 mm
System of operation: manually operated bolt
Muzzle velocity: 2,750 ft (838 m) per second
Range:
Rate of fire:
Cooling system: air
Feed system: 10-round box
Dimensions: Barrel length 27.5 in (699 mm)
          Overall length 46.5 in (1.181 m)
          Width
          Height
Weights: 9.75 lb (4.43 kg)
Sights: L1A1 telescope
Ammunition: 7.62 mm × 51
Used only by: UK
Notes: The L42A1 is a specialist sniper rifle made by adapting No 4 SMLE rifles to fire the 7.62-mm NATO round, and adding provision for a telescopic sight.

Individual Weapon

Type: selective fire assault rifle
Calibre: 4.85 mm
System of operation: gas
Muzzle velocity: 2,953 ft (900 m) per second
Range:
Rate of fire: 700 to 850 rounds per minute (cyclic)
Cooling system: air
Feed system: 20- or 30-round box
Dimensions: Barrel length 20.4 in (518.5 mm) including flash hider
          Overall length 30.3 in (770 mm)
          Width
          Height
Weights: 8.2 lb (3.72 kg) empty; 9.08 lb (4.12 kg)
Sights: × 4 SUSAT telescopic sight
Ammunition: 4.85 mm Ball
Used by: under development for trials purposes
Notes: The Individual Weapon is being developed in parallel with the Light Support Weapon, with which it shares some 80% of components. The IW differs from the LSW mainly in being shorter, and therefore having a lower muzzle velocity, and not being fitted with a bipod. There seems to be little chance that the British 4.85 mm round will be adopted as a standard NATO round, and so the production chances of the IW are slim, despite the manifest capabilities of the weapon.

THE
ROYAL
NAVY

THE ROYAL NAVY

Ships: 72 major surface combat vessels
30 major underwater combat vessels
Personnel: (at 1 April 1979) 72,900 men and women, including 7,450 Royal Marines and Fleet Air Arm (28,000 Regular and 6,500 Volunteer reservists)
Bases: Devonport, Faslane, Portland, Portsmouth and Rosyth

Strategic Forces
Nuclear-powered ballistic missile submarines
4 'Resolution' class SSBNs, each fitted with 16 Polaris A-3 SLBMs

Tactical Forces
Attack submarines
4 'Swiftsure' class SSNs
5 'Valiant' class SSNs
1 'Dreadnought' class SSN
13 'Oberon' class
3 'Porpoise' class
(2 'Trafalgar' class SSNs)*
(2 'Swiftsure' class SSNs)

ASW/Commando carriers
2 'Hermes' class

ASW cruisers
(3 'Invincible' class)

Helicopter cruisers
2 'Tiger' class

Guided-missile light cruisers
1 Type 82
7 'County' class
5 'Sheffield' class (Type 42)
(9 'Sheffield' class [Type 42])

Frigates
1 'Broadsword' class (Type 22)
8 'Amazon' class (Type 21)
26 'Leander' and 'Broad-beamed Leander' classes
7 'Tribal' class (Type 81)
8 'Rothesay' class (Modified Type 12)
1 'Leopard' class (Type 41)
1 'Salisbury' class (Type 61)
1 'Whitby' class (Type 12)
(5 'Broadsword' class [Type 22])

Assault ships
2 'Fearless' class

Mine-warfare forces
33 'Ton' class
3 'Ham' class
2 'Ley' class
(5 'Hunt' class)

Patrol forces
5 'Island' class
4 'Bird' class
5 'Ton' class
1 FPB
2 inshore patrol craft
(2 'Island' class)
(1 Boeing hydrofoil)

Hovercraft
1 VT2 class
2 SRN-6 class
1 BH-N7 class
(? VT2)

Miscellaneous include
13 survey vessels
3 depot/support ships
1 ice patrol ship
1 royal yacht/hospital ship

Guided weapons
Exocet SSM
Ikara ASWGW
Seacat SAM
Seaslug SAM
Sea Dart SAM
Seawolf SAM
(Sea Skua ASM)
(Sub-Harpoon USGW)

Fleet Air Arm
ASW helicopter squadrons
5 with 31 Sea King HAS.2 and HAS.2A
1 with 36 Wasp HAS.1
1 with 16 Wessex HAS.3
1 with 18 Lynx HAS.2

commando assault helicopter squadrons
2 with 24 Wessex HU.5

SAR/training helicopter squadrons
6 with 11 Wessex HAS.1; 23 Wessex HU.5; 13 Sea King HAS.1, HAS.2 and HAS.2A; 11 Wasp HAS.1; and 18 Gazelle HT.2

Intensive Flight Trials Unit
1 with Sea Harrier FRS.1

communications units
1 squadron and 3 flights with 3 Sea Heron C.3; 1 Heron C.4; 5 Sea Devon C.20; 1 Devon C.2/2; 3 Chipmunk T.40; and 5 Wessex HU.5

training units
1 observer training squadron with 6 Jetstream T.2 and 6 Sea Prince
1 training flight with 9 Chipmunk T.10

fleet requirements and direction training unit
1 with 12 Canberra T.4, Canberra TT.18 and Canberra T.22, and 21 Hunter T.8

(34 Sea Harrier FRS.1 and T.4)
(10 Jetstream T.2)
(2 Hunter T.8)
(21 Sea King HAS.2)
(15 Sea King HC.4)
(30 Lynx HAS.2)

Royal Marines
Commando brigade
1 with 4 commando groups, 1 light helicopter squadron and support units

Equipment
120-mm Wombat RCLs
Blowpipe SAM
Milan ATGW
SS.11 ATGW
12 Gazelle AH.1
6 Scout AH.1
(4 Lynx)

* Equipment within brackets is on order

'Resolution' class nuclear ballistic missile submarine (4)

Class: *Resolution* (S22), *Repulse* (S23), *Renown* (S26), *Revenge* (S27)
Displacement: 7,500 tons (7,620 tonnes) surfaced; 8,400 tons (8,534 tonnes) dived
Dimensions: Length 425 ft (129.5 m)
Beam 33 ft (10.1 m)
Draught 30 ft (9.1 m)
Armament:
Guns none
Missile systems
16 Polaris A-3 SLBM launchers
A/S weapons
none
Torpedo tubes
6 21-in (533-mm)
Aircraft
none
Radar and electronics: I-band search radar
Sonar: Types 2001 and 2007
Powerplant: 1 pressurised water-cooled reactor, supplying steam to geared turbines, delivering power to one shaft
Speed: 20 knots (surfaced); 25 knots (dived)
Range: limited only by food capacity and crew efficiency
Crew: 13+130 (two crews)
Used only by: UK
Notes: The first pair were built between 1964 and 1967 by Vickers (Shipbuilding) at Barrow-in-Furness, being commissioned in 1967 and 1968; the second pair were built between 1964 and 1968 by Cammell Laird at Birkenhead, being commissioned in 1968 and 1969. The boats each have two crews to ensure maximum sea time.

'Swiftsure' class nuclear attack submarine (6)

Class: *Sceptre* (S104), *Sovereign* (S108), *Superb* (S109), *Spartan* (S111), *Severn* (S112), *Swiftsure* (S126)
Displacement: 4,200 tons (4,267 tonnes) standard; 4,500 tons (4,572 tonnes) dived
Dimensions: Length 272 ft (82.9 m)
Beam 32 ft 4 in (9.8 m)
Draught 27 ft (8.2 m)
Armament:
Guns none
Missile systems
none
A/S weapons
none
Torpedo tubes
5 21-in (533-mm) with 25 torpedoes
Aircraft
none
Radar and electronics: Type 1003 search radar
Sonar: Type 2001, Type 2007, Type 197 and Type 183
Powerplant: 1 pressurised water-cooled reactor supplying steam to English Electric geared turbines, delivering power to one shaft
Speed: 30 knots (dived)
Range: limited only by food capacity and crew efficiency
Crew: 12+85
Used only by: UK

Notes: All the boats of this class are of Vickers (Shipbuilding) construction at Barrow-in-Furness. The first boat, *Swiftsure,* was laid down in 1969, and the last, *Severn,* in 1976. *Swiftsure* was commissioned in 1973, *Sovereign* in 1974, *Superb* in 1976, and *Sceptre* in 1978. *Spartan* and *Severn* will probably be commissioned in 1980 and 1981.

'Valiant' class nuclear attack submarine (5)

Class: *Churchill* (S46), *Conqueror* (S48), *Courageous* (S50), *Valiant* (S102), *Warspite* (S103)
Displacement: 4,400 tons (4,470 tonnes) standard; 4,900 tons (4,978 tonnes) full load
Dimensions: Length 285 ft (86.9 m)
Beam 33 ft 3 in (10.1 m)
Draught 27 ft (8.2 m)
Armament:
Guns none
Missile systems
none
A/S weapons
none
Torpedo tubes
6 21-in (533-mm) with 32 torpedoes
Aircraft
none
Radar and electronics: Type 1003 search radar
Sonar: Type 2001, Type 2007, Type 197 and Type 183
Powerplant: 1 pressurised water-cooled reactor supplying steam to English Electric geared turbines, delivering power to one shaft
Speed: 28 knots (dived)
Range: limited only by food capacity and crew efficiency
Crew: 13+90
Used only by: UK
Notes: *Conqueror* was built by Cammell Laird at Birkenhead, the others by Vickers (Shipbuilding) at Barrow-in-Furness. The first boat, *Valiant,* was laid down in 1962, launched in 1963, and commissioned in 1966; the last boat, *Courageous,* in 1968, 1970, and 1971.

'Dreadnought' class nuclear attack submarine (1)

Class: *Dreadnought* (S101)
Displacement: 3,000 tons (3,048 tonnes) standard; 3,500 tons (3,556 tonnes) surfaced; 4,000 tons (4,064 tonnes) dived
Dimensions: Length 265 ft 9 in (81.0 m)
Beam 32 ft 3 in (9.8 m)
Draught 26 ft (7.9 m)
Armament:
Guns none
Missile systems
none
A/S weapons
none
Torpedo tubes
6 21-in (533-mm)
Aircraft
none
Radar and electronics: I-band search radar
Sonar: Type 2001 and Type 2007
Powerplant: 1 Westinghouse S5W pressurised water-cooled reactor, supplying steam to geared turbines, delivering power to one shaft
Speed: 28 knots (dived)
Range: limited only by food capacity and crew efficiency
Crew: 11+77
Used only by: UK
Notes: *Dreadnought* was the UK's first nuclear-powered submarine, and was built between 1959 and 1960 by Vickers-Armstrong at Barrow-in-Furness. She was commissioned in 1963.

'Oberon' and 'Porpoise' class submarine (17)

Class: *Porpoise* (S01), *Finwhale* (S05), *Sealion* (S07), *Walrus* (S08), *Oberon* (S09), *Odin* (S10), *Orpheus* (S11), *Olympus* (S12), *Osiris* (S13), *Onslaught* (S14), *Otter* (S15), *Oracle* (S16), *Ocelot* (S17), *Otus* (S18), *Opossum* (S19), *Opportune* (S20), *Onyx* (S21)
Displacement: 1,610 tons (1,636 tonnes) standard; 2,030 tons (2,062 tonnes) surfaced; 2,410 tons (2,449 tonnes) dived
Dimensions: Length 295 ft 3 in (90.0 m)
Beam 26 ft 6 in (8.1 m)
Draught 18 ft (5.5 m)
Armament:
Guns none

Missile systems
none
A/S weapons
none
Torpedo tubes
8 21-in (533-mm) with 24 torpedoes
Aircraft
none
Radar and electronics: I-band search radar
Sonar: Types 186 and 187

Powerplant: 2 Admiralty Standard Range diesels, delivering 3,680 bhp, and 2 electric motors, delivering 6,000 shp to two shafts
Speed: 12 knots (surfaced); 17 knots (dived)
Range:
Crew: 6+65 in 'Porpoise' class; 6+62 in 'Oberon' class
Used also by: Australia, Brazil, Canada, Chile

Notes: The four boats of the 'Porpoise' class and 13 boats of the 'Oberon' class were built by a number of yards, the 'Porpoise' class being built between 1954 and 1958, commissioning between 1958 and 1961, and the 'Oberon' class being built between 1957 and 1964, commissioning between 1961 and 1967.

'Hermes' class helicopter/VTOL carrier (2)

Class: *Hermes* (R12), *Bulwark* (R08)
Displacement: 23,900 tons (24,282 tonnes) standard; 28,700 tons (29,159 tonnes) full load
Dimensions: Length 744 ft 4 in (226.7 m)
Beam (hull) 90 ft (27.4 m)
Draught 29 ft (8.8 m)
Armament:
Guns none
Missile systems
2 quadruple Seacat SAM launchers
A/S weapons
none
Torpedo tubes
none
Aircraft
13 helicopters
Radar and electronics: Type 965 surveillance, Type 993 search, Type 1006 navigation, and GWS 22 fire-control radars
Sonar:
Powerplant: 4 Admiralty boilers supplying steam to Parsons geared turbines, delivering 76,000 shp to two shafts
Speed: 28 knots
Range:
Crew: 980
Used only by: UK
Notes: *Hermes* was built between 1944 and 1953 by Vickers-Armstrong at Barrow-in-Furness, and commissioned in 1959. She

was modernised between 1964 and 1966, and converted into a commando carrier between 1971 and 1973. In 1976 and 1977 she was again converted, this time into an anti-submarine carrier with commando capability. The carrier *Bulwark* (R08), recommissioned in 1979 as a replacement for *Ark Royal*, is a sistership of *Hermes*.

'Invincible' class anti-submarine cruiser (3)

Class: *Invincible* (CAH1), *Illustrious* (CAH2), *Ark Royal* (CAH3)
Displacement: 16,000 tons (16,256 tonnes) standard; 19,500 tons (19,812 tonnes) full load
Dimensions: Length 677 ft (206.6 m)
Beam (deck) 104 ft 7 in (31.9 m)
Draught 24 ft (7.3 m) (?)
Armament:
Guns none
Missile systems
4 MM38 Exocet SSM launchers (possibly)
1 twin Sea Dart SAM launcher
A/S weapons
none
Torpedo tubes
none

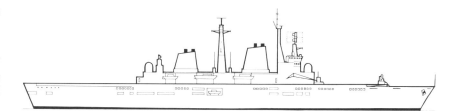

Aircraft
9 helicopters and 5 aircraft
Radar and electronics: Type 965 surveillance, Type 992R search, Type 909 fire-control, and Type 1006 navigation radars
Sonar: Type 184
Powerplant: 4 Rolls-Royce Olympus gas turbines, delivering 112,000 shp to two shafts
Speed: 28 knots
Range: 5,000 miles (8,047 km) at 18 knots

Crew: 31+869 (excluding aircrew)
Used by: building for UK
Notes: *Invincible* was built by Vickers at Barrow-in-Furness between 1973 and 1977, and is scheduled for commissioning in 1979. *Illustrious* was laid down in 1976 at the Wallsend-on-Tyne yard of Swan Hunter. There are indications that a third ship of the class may be ordered.

'Tiger' class helicopter cruiser (2)

Class: *Tiger* (C20), ex-*Bellerophon*; *Blake* (C99), ex-*Tiger*, ex-*Blake*
Displacement: 9,500 tons (9,652 tonnes) standard; 12,080 tons (12,273 tonnes) full load

Dimensions: Length 566 ft 6 in (172.8 m)
Beam 64 ft (19.5 m)
Draught 23 ft (7.0 m)
Armament:
Guns 2 6-in (152-mm) in a twin turret
2 3-in (76-mm) in a twin turret
Missile systems
2 quadruple Seacat SAM launchers

A/S weapons
none
Torpedo tubes
none
Aircraft
4 helicopters
Radar and electronics: Types 965 and 993 search, Type 277 or 278 height-finder,

MRS 3 fire-control, and Type 978 navigation radars

Sonar:

Powerplant: 4 Admiralty boilers supplying steam to 4 Parsons geared turbines, delivering 80,000 shp to four shafts

Speed: 30 knots

Range: 4,000 miles (6,440 km) at 20 knots

Crew: 85+800

Used only by: UK

Notes: *Tiger* was built between 1941 and 1945 by John Brown on Clydebank, and commissioned in 1959; *Blake* was built between 1942 and 1945 by Fairfield Ship-

building & Engineering at Govan, and commissioned in 1961. Designed and laid down as conventional cruisers, the ships were suspended in construction in 1946, and restarted in 1954, when work was further delayed by redesign.

Type 82 light cruiser (1)

Class: *Bristol* (D23)

Displacement: 6,100 tons (6,198 tonnes) standard; 7,100 tons (7,214 tonnes) full load

Dimensions: Length 507 ft (154.5 m)
Beam 55 ft (16.8 m)
Draught 23 ft (7.0 m) to bottom of sonar dome

Armament:

Guns 1 4.5-in (114-mm)

Missile systems

1 twin Sea Dart SAM launcher

A/S weapons

1 Ikara launcher

1 3-barrel Limbo mortar

Torpedo tubes

Aircraft

facilities for 1 small helicopter

Radar and electronics: Type 965 surveillance, Type 992 search, Type 909 fire-control, and Types 1006 and 978 navigation radars; Action Data Automation Weapon System

Sonar: Types 162, 170, 182, 184, 185 and 189

Powerplant: COSAG (COmbined Steam And Gas turbine) arrangement with 2 boilers supplying steam to 2 Standard Range geared turbines, delivering 30,000 shp,

and 2 Bristol Siddeley Marine Olympus TMIA gas turbines delivering 56,000 shp to two shafts

Speed: 30 knots

Range: 5,000 miles (8,047 km) at 18 knots

Crew: 29+378

Used only by: UK

Notes: *Bristol* was built between 1967 and 1969 by Swan Hunter & Tyne Shipbuilders, and commissioned in 1973. She is officially rated as a destroyer, with some justification.

'County' class light cruiser (7)

Class: *Devonshire* (D02), *Kent* (D12), *London* (D16), *Antrim* (D18), *Glamorgan* (D19), *Fife* (D20), *Norfolk* (D21)

Displacement: 5,440 tons (5,527 tonnes) standard; 6,200 tons (6,299 tonnes) full load

Dimensions: Length 520 ft 6 in (158.7 m)
Beam 54 ft (16.5 m)
Draught 20 ft (6.1 m)

Armament:

Guns 4 (*Devonshire*, *Kent* and *London*) or 2 (others) 4.5-in (114-mm) in twin turrets
2 20-mm in single mountings

Missile systems

4 MM38 Exocet SSM launchers in *Antrim*, *Glamorgan*, *Fife* and *Norfolk*
1 twin Seaslug SAM launcher
2 quadruple Seacat SAM launchers

A/S weapons

Torpedo tubes

Aircraft

1 helicopter

Radar and electronics: Type 965 air search, Type 992 surveillance, Type 277 height-finder, Type 901 Seaslug fire-control, MRS 3 gun fire-control, GWS 21 (*Devonshire* and *London*) or GWS 22 (others) Seacat fire-control radars

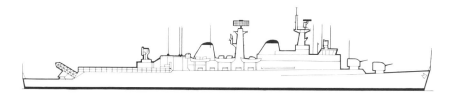

Sonar:
Powerplant: COSAG (COmbined Steam And Gas turbine) arrangement, with 2 Babcock & Wilcox boilers supplying steam to 2 geared turbines, delivering 30,000 shp, and 4 G.6 gas turbines, delivering 30,000 shp to two shafts

Speed: 30 knots
Range:
Crew: 33+438
Used only by: UK
Notes: The ships were built by five yards in the period between 1959 and 1967, and commissioned between 1962 and 1970. Their sistership *Hampshire* has been paid off for financial reasons. The vessels are officially described as destroyers.

Type 42 ('Sheffield' class) destroyer (10 + 4)

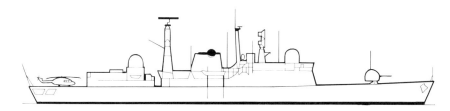

Class: *Sheffield* (D80), *Birmingham* (D86), *Newcastle* (D87), *Glasgow* (D88), *Cardiff* (D108), *Coventry* (D118), *Exeter* (D89), *Southampton* (D90), *Nottingham* (D91), *Liverpool* (D92)
Displacement: 3,150 tons (3,200 tonnes) standard; 4,100 tons (4,166 tonnes) full load
Dimensions: Length 410 ft (125.0 m)
Beam 46 ft (14.0 m)
Draught 14 ft (4.3 m)
Armament:
Guns 1 4.5-in (114-mm)
2 20-mm
Missile systems
1 twin Sea Dart SAM launcher
A/S weapons
2 triple 12.75-in (324-mm) tubes
Torpedo tubes
none
Aircraft
1 ASW helicopter

Radar and electronics: Type 965 search, Type 992Q surveillance and target indicator, Type 909 SAM fire-control, and Type 1006 navigation radars; ADAWS 4 action data automation and weapons system
Sonar: Types 184 and 162
Powerplant: COGOG (COmbined Gas turbines Or Gas turbine) arrangement, with 2 Rolls-Royce Olympus gas turbines, delivering 50,000 shp, and 2 Rolls-Royce Tyne gas turbines, delivering 8,000 shp to two shafts
Speed: 30 knots
Range: 4,500 miles (7,245 km) at 18 knots
Crew: 26+273

Used also by: Argentina
Notes: The ships have been built by several yards in the period between 1970 and 1976, the first six ships being commissioned in the period from 1975 to 1978. *Exeter* and *Southampton* are building in the yards of Swan Hunter at Wallsend-on-Tyne and Vosper Thornycroft, and *Nottingham* has been ordered from the Vosper Thornycroft yard, and a tenth unit from Cammell Laird, Birkenhead.

Type 21 ('Amazon' class) guided missile frigate (8)

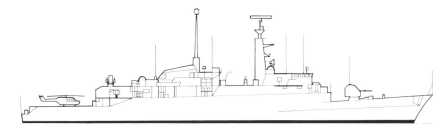

Class: *Amazon* (F169), *Antelope* (F170), *Active* (F171), *Ambuscade* (F172), *Arrow* (F173), *Alacrity* (F174), *Ardent* (F184), *Avenger* (F185)
Displacement: 2,750 tons (2,794 tonnes) standard; 3,250 tons (3,302 tonnes) full load
Dimensions: Length 384 ft (117.0 m)
Beam 41 ft 9 in (12.7 m)
Draught 14 ft 6 in (4.4 m)
Armament:
Guns 1 4.5-in (114-mm)
2 20-mm in single mountings

Missile systems
4 MM38 Exocet SSM launchers
1 quadruple Seacat SAM launcher (Seawolf to be retrofitted)
A/S weapons
2 triple 12.75-in (324-mm) tubes to be fitted

Torpedo tubes
none
Aircraft
1 ASW helicopter
Radar and electronics: Type 992Q surveillance and target indicator, GWS 24 SAM fire-control, Orion RTN-10X WSA 4 gun

fire-control, and Type 978 navigation radars; CAAIS
Sonar: Type 184M and Type 162M
Powerplant: COGOG (COmbined Gas turbine Or Gas turbine) arrangement, with 2 Rolls-Royce Olympus gas turbines, delivering 56,000 shp, and 2 Rolls-Royce Tyne gas turbines, delivering 8,500 shp to two shafts
Speed: 32 knots
Range: 3,500 miles (5,635 km) at 18 knots
Crew: 13+164
Used only by: UK

Notes: The class was designed by Vosper Thornycroft, and built by them (first three) and by Yarrow at Glasgow (last five), in the period between 1969 and 1975, with commissioning in the period between 1974 and 1978.

Type 22 ('Broadsword' class) guided missile frigate (5)

Class: *Broadsword* (F88), *Battleaxe* (F89), *Brilliant* (F90), *Brazen* (F91), *Boxer* (F92)
Displacement: 3,500 tons (3,556 tonnes) standard; 4,000 tons (4,064 tonnes) full load
Dimensions: Length 430 ft (131.2 m)
Beam 48 ft 6 in (14.8 m)
Draught 14 ft (4.3 m)
Armament:
Guns 2 40-mm
Missile systems
1 quadruple MM38 Exocet SSM launcher
2 Sea Wolf SAM launchers
A/S weapons
2 triple 12.75-in (324-mm) Mark 32 tubes
Torpedo tubes
none
Aircraft
2 ASW helicopters
Radar and electronics: Type 967/8 surveillance, Type 1006 and Type 910 tracker radars
Sonar: Type 2016
Powerplant: COGOG (COmbined Gas turbine Or Gas turbine) arrangement, with 2 Rolls-Royce Olympus gas turbines, delivering 56,000 bhp, and 2 Rolls-Royce Tyne gas turbines, delivering 8,500 bhp to two shafts

Speed: 30+ knots
Range: 4,500 miles (7,245 km) at 18 knots on Tynes
Crew: about 250
Used by: building for UK
Notes: The 'Broadsword' class, of which some 14 ships are planned, is to be the successor to the 'Leander' class. The four present ships are of Yarrow construction, with *Broadsword* entering service in 1979. Intended mainly for A/S operations, the class is notable for its lack of gun armament except for a pair of 40-mm AA weapons

'Leander' and 'Broad-beamed Leander' class frigate (26)

Class: *Aurora* (F10), *Euryalus* (F15), *Galatea* (F18), *Cleopatra* (F28), *Arethusa* (F38), *Naiad* (F39), *Sirius* (F40), *Phoebe* (F42), *Minerva* (F45), *Danae* (F47), *Juno* (F52), *Argonaut* (F56), *Dido* (F104), *Leander* (F109), *Ajax* (F114), *Penelope* (F127); *Achilles* (F12), *Diomede* (F16), *Andromeda* (F57), *Hermione* (F58), *Jupiter* (F60), *Bacchante* (F69), *Apollo* (F70), *Scylla* (F71), *Ariadne* (F72), *Charybdis* (F75)
Displacement: 2,450 tons (2,489 tonnes) standard and 2,860 tons (2,906 tonnes) full load for 'Leander'; 2,500 tons (2,540 tonnes) standard and 2,962 tons (3,009 tonnes) full load for 'Broad-beamed Leander'
Dimensions: Length 373 ft (113.4 m)
Beam 41 ft (12.5 m) for 'Leander'; 43 ft (13.1 m) for 'Broad-beamed Leander'
Draught 18 ft (5.5 m)
Armament:
Guns 2 4.5-in (114-mm) in a twin turret
2 40-mm (generally)
2 20-mm (in ships fitted with Seacat)
Missile systems
4 MM38 Exocet SSM launchers (in place of 4.5-in/114-mm guns) in 'Broad-beamed Leanders', *Cleopatra, Sirius, Phoebe, Minerva, Juno, Argonaut, Dido, Danae*
1 quadruple Seacat SAM launcher, except Ikara ships (2 quadruple Seacat SAM launchers) and Exocet ships (3 quadruple Seacat SAM launchers)
A/S weapons
1 Ikara launcher (in place of 4.5-in/114-mm guns) in *Leander, Ajax, Galatea, Naiad, Euryalus, Aurora, Arethusa, Penelope*
1 3-barrel Limbo mortar (not Exocet ships)
2 triple 12.75-in (324-mm) Mark 32 tubes (Exocet ships only)
Torpedo tubes
none
Aircraft
1 small helicopter
Radar and electronics: Type 965 surveillance (not Ikara ships), Type 993 combined air/surface warning, MRS 3/GWS 22 fire-control, and Types 978 or 1006 (rebuilt ships) navigation radars
Sonar: Type 199 variable-depth in Ikara ships
Powerplant: 2 boilers supplying steam to 2 double-reduction geared turbines, delivering 30,000 shp to two shafts

Speed: 30 knots
Range:
Crew: 251 ('Leander'); 260 ('Broad-beamed Leander')
Used also by: Chile, India, New Zealand
Notes: The 'Leander' class was developed from the 'Rothesay' class, and its ships were built in a number of yards from 1959 to 1971. The first unit, *Leander,* was commissioned in March 1963, and the last, *Ariadne,* in February 1973. There are 16 of the original 'Leander' class, and 10 of the improved 'Broad-beamed Leander' class.

Type 81 ('Tribal' class) frigate (7)

Class: *Ashanti* (F117), *Eskimo* (F118), *Gurkha* (F122), *Zulu* (F124), *Mohawk* (F125), *Nubian* (F131), *Tartar* (F133)
Displacement: 2,300 tons (2,337 tonnes) standard; 2,700 tons (2,743 tonnes) full load
Dimensions: Length 360 ft (109.7 m)
Beam 42 ft 4 in (12.9 m)
Draught 17 ft 6 in (5.3 m)
Armament:
Guns 2 4.5-in (114-mm) in single turrets
2 20-mm
Missile systems
2 quadruple Seacat SAM launchers
A/S weapons
1 3-barrel Limbo mortar
Torpedo tubes
none
Aircraft
1 small helicopter
Radar and electronics: Type 965 search, Type 293 combined air/surface warning, MRS 3 gun fire-control, GWS 21 SAM fire-control, and Type 978 navigation radars

Sonar: Types 177, 170 and 162, plus Type 199 variable-depth in *Ashanti* and *Gurkha*
Powerplant: COSAG (COmbined Steam And Gas turbine) arrangement, with 2 Babcock & Wilcox boilers supplying steam to 1 Metrovick turbine, delivering 12,500 shp, and 1 Metrovick gas turbine, delivering 7,500 shp to one shaft
Speed: 28 knots
Range:

Crew: 13+240
Used only by: UK
Notes: The seven ships of the 'Tribal' class were designed for distant operations, in which a fair measure of self-sufficiency and great range would be needed. The ships were built by seven different yards between 1958 and 1962, being commissioned between 1961 and 1964.

Modified Type 12 ('Rothesay' class) frigate (9)

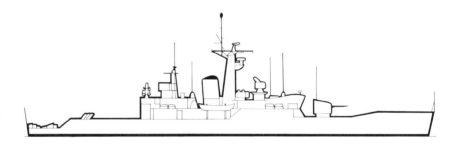

Class: *Yarmouth* (F101), *Lowestoft* (F103), *Brighton* (F106), *Rothesay* (F107), *Londonderry* (F108), *Falmouth* (F113), *Berwick* (F115), *Plymouth* (F126), *Rhyl* (F129)
Displacement: 2,380 tons (2,418 tonnes) standard; 2,800 tons (2,845 tonnes) full load
Dimensions: Length 370 ft (112.8 m)
Beam 41 ft (12.5 m)
Draught 17 ft 4 in (5.3 m)
Armament:
Guns 2 4.5-in (114-mm) in a twin turret
2 20-mm in single mountings
Missile systems
1 quadruple Seacat SAM launcher
A/S weapons
1 3-barrel Limbo mortar
Torpedo tubes
none

Aircraft
1 small helicopter
Radar and electronics: Type 993 search, MRS 3 fire-control, and Type 978 navigation radars
Sonar:
Powerplant: 2 Babcock & Wilcox boilers supplying steam to 2 Admiralty Standard Range double-reduction geared turbines, delivering 30,000 shp to two shafts

Speed: 30 knots
Range:
Crew: 15+220
Used only by: UK
Notes: The nine ships of the class were built in eight yards in the period between 1956 and 1960, being commissioned in 1960 and 1961. The design was based on that of the 'Whitby' class.

Type 61 ('Salisbury' class) frigate (2)

Class: *Salisbury* (F32), *Lincoln* (F99)
Displacement: 2,170 tons (2,205 tonnes) standard; 2,408 tons (2,447 tonnes) full load
Dimensions: Length 339 ft 9 in (103.6 m)
Beam 40 ft (12.2 m)
Draught 15 ft 6 in (4.7 m)
Armament:
Guns 2 4.5-in (114-mm) in a twin turret
2 20-mm
Missile systems
1 quadruple Seacat SAM launcher
A/S weapons
1 3-barrel Squid mortar
Torpedo tubes
none
Aircraft
none
Radar and electronics: Type 965 long-range surveillance. Type 993 combined air/surface warning, Type 277Q height-finder. Type 982 target indicator. Type 275 (Mark 6M director) fire-control, and Type 978 navi-

gation radars; Knebworth Corvus chaff dispensers
Sonar: Types 174 and 170B
Powerplant: 8 Admiralty Standard Range diesels, delivering 14,400 bhp to two shafts
Speed: 24 knots
Range: 7,500 miles (12,070 km) at 16 knots
Crew: 14+223
Used also by: Bangladesh

Notes: *Salisbury* was built by Devonport Dockyard, *Lincoln* by Fairfield Shipbuilding & Engineering at Govan, between 1955 and 1959, for commissioning in 1960. The class is intended primarily to provide direction for strike aircraft. Their sistership *Llandaff* was transferred to Bangladesh in 1976.

Type 12 ('Whitby' class) frigate (1)

Class: *Torquay* (F43)
Displacement: 2,150 tons (2,184 tonnes) standard; 2,560 tons (2,601 tonnes) full load
Dimensions: Length 369 ft 9 in (112.7 m)
  Beam 41 ft (12.5 m)
  Draught 17 ft (5.2 m)
Armament:
Guns 2 4.5-in (114-mm) in a twin turret
Missile systems
  none
A/S weapons
  13-barrel Limbo mortar
Torpedo tubes
  none
Aircraft
  none
Radar and electronics: Type 993 search, Type 275 fire-control, and Type 1006 navigation radars
Sonar: Types 174, 170 and 162
Powerplant: 2 Babcock & Wilcox boilers supplying steam to 2 double-reduction geared turbines, delivering 30,430 shp to two shafts
Speed: 31 knots
Range:
Crew: 12+213
Used also by: Bangladesh, India, New Zealand
Notes: *Torquay* was built between 1953 and 1954 by Harland & Wolff at Belfast, for commissioning in 1956. She is now used as a navigation/direction trials and training ship.

Assault ship (2)

Class: *Fearless* (L10), *Intrepid* (L11)
Displacement: 11,060 tons (11,237 tonnes) standard; 12,120 tons (12,314 tonnes) full load
Dimensions: Length 520 ft (158.5 m)
  Beam 80 ft (24.4 m)
  Draught 20 ft 6 in (6.2 m)
Armament:
Guns 2 40-mm Bofors
Missile systems
  4 quadruple Seacat SAM launchers
A/S weapons
  none
Torpedo tubes
  none
Aircraft
  facilities for 5 helicopters
Radar and electronics: Type 993 air/surface search and Type 978 navigation radars; Computer Assisted Action Information System (CAAIS); Knebworth Corvus chaff dispensers
Sonar:
Powerplant: 2 Babcock & Wilcox boilers supplying steam to 2 English Electric turbines, delivering 22,000 shp to two shafts
Speed: 21 knots
Range: 5,000 miles (8,047 km) at 20 knots
Crew: 580
Used only by: UK
Notes: The ships were built by Harland & Wolff in Belfast and John Brown on Clydebank, between 1962 and 1964, for commissioning in 1965 and 1967. Each ship can carry up to 700 troops, 15 tanks and up to 30 other vehicles, landed by the ship's four LCM(9)s in the dock and four LCVPs at the davits. The dock at the rear of the ship is flooded by flooding down the stern to a draught of 32 ft (9.8 m). Only one ship is kept in commission at any one time.

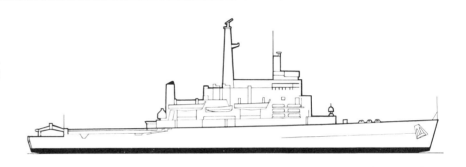

'Ton' class minehunter and mine-sweeper (33)

Class: *Bildeston* (M1110), *Brereton* (M1113), *Brinton* (M1114), *Bronington* (M1140), *Hubberston* (M1147), *Iveston* (M1151), *Kedleston* (M1153), *Kellington* (M1154), *Kirkliston* (M1157), *Maxton* (M1165), *Nurton* (M1166), *Sheraton* (M1181) and *Shoulton* (M1182); *Alfriston* (M1103), *Bickington* (M1109), *Crichton* (M1124), *Cuxton* (M1125), *Glasserton* (M1141), *Hodgeston* (M1146), *Laleston* (M1158), *Repton* (M1167), *Pollington* (M1173), *Shavington* (M1180), *Upton* (M1187), *Walkerton* (M1188), *Wotton* (M1195), *Soberton* (M1200), *Stubbington* (M1204), *Wiston* (M1205), *Lewiston* (M1208) and *Crofton* (M1216)

Displacement: 360 tons (365.8 tonnes) standard; 425 tons (431.8 tonnes) full load

Dimensions: Length 153 ft (46.3 m)
Beam 28 ft 9 in (8.8 m)
Draught 8 ft 3 in (2.5 m)

Armament:
Guns very varied, most minehunters having 1 or 2 40-mm and 2 20-mm, and mine-sweepers 0 or 1 40-mm
Missile systems
none
A/S weapons
none
Torpedo tubes
none

Aircraft
none
Radar and electronics: Type 975
Sonar: Type 193 in minehunters
Powerplant: 2 JVSS 12 Mirlees diesels, delivering 2,500 bhp, or 2 Napier 18A-7A Deltic diesels, delivering 3,000 bhp to two shafts
Speed: 15 knots
Range: 2,300 miles (3,700 km) at 13 knots
Crew: 29 (minesweeper); 5 + 33 (minehunter)

Used also by: Argentina, Eire, Ghana, India, Malaysia, South Africa
Notes: Some 118 of these craft were originally built between 1953 and 1960, by a number of yards under the directorship of John I. Thornycroft of Southampton. The first 15 ships above are minehunters, the remaining 17 minesweepers. *Kedleston*, *Kellington*, *Hodgeston*, *Repton*, *Upton* and *Crofton* are used as Royal Naval Reserve training ships.

'Island' class offshore patrol craft (5)

Class: *Jersey* (P295), *Guernsey* (P297), *Shetland* (P298), *Orkney* (P299), *Lindisfarne* (P300)
Displacement: 925 tons (939.8 tonnes) standard; 1,250 tons (1,270 tonnes) full load
Dimensions: Length 195 ft 4 in (59.6 m)
Beam 35 ft 9 in (10.9 m)
Draught 14 ft (4.3 m)

Armament:
Guns 1 40-mm
Missile systems
none
A/S weapons
none
Torpedo tubes
none
Aircraft
none
Radar and electronics: Type 1006 navigation radar

Sonar:
Powerplant: 2 diesels, delivering 4,380 hp to one shaft
Speed: 16 knots
Range: 7,000 miles (11,265 km) at 15 knots
Crew: 34
Used only by: UK
Notes: All five craft were built by Hall Russell & Co. *Jersey* was commissioned in 1976 and the others in 1977–78. Two more units were ordered in 1977.

'Bird' class large patrol craft (4)

Class: *Kingfisher* (P260), *Cygnet* (P261), *Peterel* (P262), *Sandpiper* (P263)
Displacement: 190 tons (193 tonnes)
Dimensions: Length 120 ft (36.6 m)
Beam 23 ft (7.0 m)
Draught 6 ft 6 in (2.0 m)
Armament:
Guns 1 40-mm
2 machine-guns
Missile systems
none
A/S weapons
none
Torpedo tubes
none
Aircraft
none
Radar and electronics: Type 1006 navigation radar
Sonar:
Powerplant: 2 Paxman 16YJ diesels, delivering 4,800 bhp
Speed: 18 knots
Range:
Crew: 24
Used only by: UK
Notes: All four craft were built by R. Dunston Ltd at Hessle, the first craft being commissioned in 1975, the next two in 1976, and the last in 1977. The design is based

on that of the RAF's 'Seal' class rescue craft, with modifications to improve sea-keeping qualities.

Aérospatiale MM38 Exocet

Type: naval surface-to-surface missile
Guidance: inertial plus active radar terminal homing
Dimensions: Span 39¾ in (100.4 cm)
Body diameter 13⅘ in (35.0 cm)
Length 17 ft 1 in (5.21 m)
Booster: SNPE Epervier solid-propellant rocket
Sustainer: SNPE Eole V solid-propellant rocket
Warhead: 364 lb (165 kg) high explosive
Weights: Launch 1,620 lb (735 kg)
Burnt out
Performance: speed Mach 0.93; range 26 miles (42 km)
Used also by: various nations
Notes: A powerful anti-ship system, the MM38 Exocet is launched by the parent ship's fire-control computer, then flies at very low level at high subsonic speed in the predetermined direction of the target, before homing in the terminal phases of the flight under the guidance of the active radar head. There are two variants of the MM38 Exocet:
1. AM39 Exocet air-launched anti-ship missile, with a length of 15 ft 4⅔ in (4.69 m), a weight of 1,433 lb (650 kg), and a range of up to 31 miles (50 km)
2. MM40 Exocet, a version with improved range (up to 43½ miles/70 km), a length of 18 ft 6⅔ in (5.65 m), and a weight of 1,819 lb (825 kg).

British Aerospace (HSD) Sea Dart

Type: naval surface-to-air tactical guided missile
Guidance: radar guidance with semi-active radar terminal homing
Dimensions: Span 36 in (91.4 cm)
Body diameter 16½ in (41.9 cm)
Length 14 ft 5¼ in (4.4 m)
Booster: solid-propellant rocket
Sustainer: Rolls-Royce Odin ramjet
Warhead: probably high explosive
Weights: Launch 1,213 lb (550 kg)
Burnt out
Performance: speed Mach 3.5; range more than 50 miles (80 km)
Used also by: Argentina
Notes: The Sea Dart system is highly flexible, and provides its parent vessels with protection against aircraft attack from anywhere between very high and very low levels. The system can also be used against missiles and other ships. Sea Dart is used with Type 919 target tracking and illuminating radar. The system is currently being updated to improve its immunity to ECM.

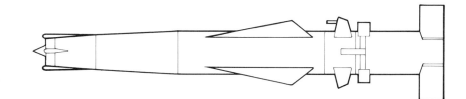

British Aerospace (HSD) Seaslug

Type: naval surface-to-air tactical guided missile, with surface-to-surface capability
Guidance: beam-riding
Dimensions: Span 4 ft 8⅜ in (1.437 m)
Body diameter 16 1/16 in (40.9 cm)
Length (Mark 1) 19 ft 8 in (5.99 m); (Mark 2) 20 ft (6.1 m)
Booster: four jettisonable solid-propellant rockets
Sustainer: solid-propellant rocket
Warhead: 297-lb (135-kg) high explosive
Weights: Launch
Burnt out

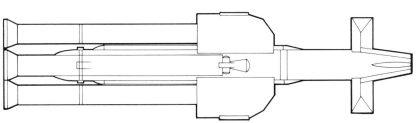

Performance: range (Mark 1) 28+ miles (45+ km), (Mark 2) 36 miles (58 km); ceiling more than 49,200 ft (15,000 m)
Used only by: UK
notes: Designed as a long-range guided missile, the Seaslug is used with Type 901M radar for guidance, Type 965 long-range surveillance radar, Type 277 height-finding radar, and Type 901 tracking and illuminating radar. The Seaslug is fired from a twin launcher, and became operational in 1961. The system is now obsolescent.

British Aerospace (BAC) Seawolf

Type: naval short-range surface-to-air missile
Guidance: line-of-sight by means of radio command

Dimensions: Span 22 in (55.88 cm)
Body diameter $7\frac{1}{10}$ in (18.0 cm)
Length 6 ft 3 in (1.905 m)
Booster: solid-propellant rocket
Sustainer: none

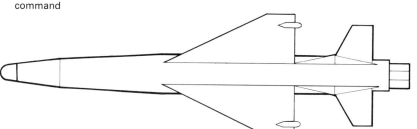

Warhead: 31-lb (14-kg) high explosive
Weights: Launch 180 lb (82 kg)
Burnt out
Performance: speed Mach 2; range 4 miles (6.4 km)
Used by: under development for UK
Notes: The Seawolf is the missile component of the Guided Weapon System 25, and is designed for the close-range air defence of ships displacing 2,000 tons (2032 tonnes) or more. It is used in conjunction with the Types 967 and 968 air and low-altitude surveillance, Type 910 tracker radars, plus a variety of TV and other installations. The missile is fired from a six-round launcher. Various other models of the missile are under development.

Short Brothers Seacat

Type: naval surface-to-air tactical guided missile
Guidance: radio command
Dimensions: Span $25\frac{1}{2}$ in (64.77 cm)
Body diameter $7\frac{1}{2}$ in (19.05 cm)
Length 4 ft 10 in (1.48 m)
Booster: solid-propellant rocket
Sustainer: solid-propellant rocket
Warhead: high explosive
Weights: Launch about 143 lb (65 kg)
Burnt out
Performance: range 4 miles (6.5 km)
Used also by: Argentina, Australia, Brazil, Chile, India, Iran, Libya, Malaysia, Netherlands, New Zealand, Sweden, Thailand, Venezuela, West Germany and others
Notes: Designed as a close-range ship-borne missile system, the Seacat was at first provided with optical sighting arrangements, in which the operator gathered the missile into his field of vision and then guided it onto the target with his thumb control. Later versions, however, have been combined with a number of naval fire-control systems.

Lockheed UGM-27C Polaris A-3

Type: two-stage submarine-launched ballistic strategic missile
Guidance: Massachusetts Institute of Technology/General Electric/Hughes intertial
Dimensions: Body diameter 4 ft 6 in (1.37 m)
Length 32 ft $3\frac{1}{4}$ in (9.85 m)
Booster (1st stage): Aerojet solid-propellant rocket
Sustainer (2nd stage): Hercules liquid-injection rocket
Warhead: nuclear, 3×200-kiloton MRVs (these are currently being updated and improved)
Weights: Launch 35,000 lb (15,876 kg)
Burnt out
Performance: range 2,875 miles (4,630 km); speed Mach 10 at burn-out; throw-weight 1,000 lb (454 kg); CEP 1,000 yards (914 m)
Used only by: UK
Notes: Final development of the Polaris SLBM, with reduced structure weight and improved propellant to improve range by a considerable margin over the Polaris A-2 (range 1,725 miles/2,780 km). The Polaris missiles on board British SSBNs have British warheads to maintain the system's credibility into the early 1990s.

Ikara

Type: guided missile carrying a homing torpedo (Mark 44 typical)
Guidance: radio command by computer with aid of sonar and radar information
Launch method: ramp
Dimensions: Length 11 ft 3 in (3.43 m)
Span 5 ft (1.52 m)
Weight:
Engine: dual-thrust solid-propellant rocket motor
Speed:
Range: about 11 miles (18 km)
Warhead: as for torpedo carried
Used also by: Australia, Brazil

Notes: Highly effective method of dispatching a torpedo to the optimum position over the target area, where it descends to the water by parachute and then homes on the submarine using its own terminal homing system. Information on the submarine's movements are fed to the shipboard computer continuously, and this latter steers the missile in flight. The launch ship's computer can also operate from information supplied by other ships and by helicopters.

Mark 20 (Improved) torpedo

Type: submarine-launched anti-ship and anti-submarine torpedo
Guidance: preset angle, course and depth, with passive sonar homing
Launch method: tube
Dimensions: Length 13 ft 6 in (4.11 m)
Diameter 21 in (533 mm)
Weight: about 1,810 lb (821 kg)
Engine: electric
Speed:
Range: 12,030 yards (11,000 m) at 20 knots
Warhead: 200 lb (91 kg) high explosive
Used only by: UK
Notes: Designed principally as an anti-submarine weapon, running at depths up to 210 ft (64 m) and homing on the propeller cavitation noise of submarines at depths of up to 800 ft (244 m). Problems with the initial guidance system have made the type none too successful.

Mark 23 torpedo

Type: submarine-launched anti-ship and anti-submarine torpedo
Guidance: wire-guidance from launch vessel, plus passive sonar homing
Launch method: tube
Dimensions: Length
Diameter 21 in (533 mm)
Weight:
Engine: electric
Speed:
Range: about 8,800 yards (8,047 m)
Warhead: 200 lb (91 kg) high explosive
Used only by: UK
Notes: Britain's first wire-guided torpedo, essentially a Mark 20 weapon with an extra section inserted for the wire casket. Intended as an interim and training weapon pending the introduction of the Mark 24, the Mark 23 is still in service as a result of delays with the Mark 24 programme.

Mark 24 'Tigerfish' torpedo

Type: submarine-launched anti-submarine torpedo
Guidance: wire-guidance from launch vessel, plus active/passive acoustic homing
Launch method: tube
Dimensions: Length 21 ft $2\frac{1}{2}$ in (6.464 m)
Diameter 21 in (533 mm)
Weight: 3,417 lb (1,550 kg)
Engine: electric
Speed: high or low speeds
Range: probably at least 20 miles (32 km)
Warhead: high explosive
Used also by: other navies
Notes: Sophisticated anti-submarine weapon, with onboard computer, roll stabilisation by means of retractable stub wings, and wire dispensed from both torpedo and launch submarine.

THE ROYAL AIR FORCE

THE ROYAL AIR FORCE

Aircraft: about 540 first-line combat aircraft

Personnel: (at 1 April 1979) 86,300 men and women (30,300 Regular and 300 RAFVR reservists)

strike/attack squadrons
  6 with 62 British Aerospace Vulcan B.2
  4 with 50 British Aerospace Buccaneer S.2A and S.2B
  6 with 72 SEPECAT Jaguar GR.1 and T.2

close-support squadrons
  3 with 60 British Aerospace Harrier GR.3 and T.4

interceptor squadrons
  7 with 85 McDonnell Douglas Phantom FGR.2 and FG.1
  2 with 43 British Aerospace Lightning F.3, F.6 and T.5 (plus 30 aircraft in reserve)

reconnaissance squadrons
  1 strategic with 4 British Aerospace Vulcan SR.2 and B.2
  2 tactical with 24 SEPECAT Jaguar GR.1 and T.2
  2 high-altitude with 20 British Aerospace Canberra B.6 and PR.9, and 3 British Aerospace Nimrod R.1

AEW squadron
  1 with 12 Avro Shackleton AEW.2

maritime reconnaissance squadrons
  4 with 31 British Aerospace Nimrod MR.1 and MR.1A

tanker squadrons
  2 with 21 Handley Page Victor K.2

strategic transport squadron
  1 with 11 British Aerospace VC10

tactical transport squadrons
  4 with 45 Lockheed C-130 Hercules C.1 (plus 10 aircraft in reserve)

communications squadrons
  3 with 6 British Aerospace 125 CC.1 and 125 CC.2, 4 British Aerospace Andover, 7 Hunting Aircraft Pembroke, 15 de Havilland Devon, 2 Westland Whirlwind and 1 Westland Gazelle

ECM/target/calibration squadrons
  4 with 58 British Aerospace Canberra B.2, E.15, T.4, T.19 and TT.18, and 6 British Aerospace Andover E.3

operational conversion units
  1 with 8 British Aerospace Vulcan B.2
  1 with 15 British Aerospace Buccaneer S.2A and S.2B
  1 with 30 SEPECAT Jaguar GR.1 and T.2
  1 with 24 McDonnell Douglas Phantom FGR.2, 8 British Aerospace Lightning F.3 and T.5, and 4 Hawker Aircraft Hunter T.7A
  1 with 19 British Aerospace Harrier GR.3 and T.4
  1 with 4 British Aerospace Nimrod MR.1
  1 with 7 British Aerospace Canberra B.2 and T.4
  1 with British Aerospace Andover and 5 Lockheed C-130 Hercules C.1
  1 with 3 Handley Page Victor K.2
  1 with 3 Westland Wessex HC.2, 5 Westland Puma C.1 and 6 Westland Sea King HAR.3

tactical weapons units
  3 with Hawker Aircraft Hunter FGA.9, F.6A and T.7, 46 British Aerospace Hawk T.1 and 2 British Aerospace Jet Provost T.4

tactical transport helicopter squadrons
  2 with 40 Westland Wessex
  2 with 31 Westland Puma HC.1

SAR helicopter squadrons
  2 with 9 Westland Whirlwinds, 9 Westland Wessex and 8 Westland Sea King

training units
  numerous, with 51 British Aerospace Hawk T.1, 141 British Aerospace Jet Provost, 17 Hawker Aircraft Hunter F.6 and T.7, 9 British Aerospace Jetstream T.1, 108 British Aerospace Bulldog T.1, 50 de Havilland Canada Chipmunk T.10, 18 British Aerospace Dominie T.1, 10 Folland Gnat T.1, 1 Beagle-Auster Husky T.1, 14 Westland Whirlwind, 5 Westland Wessex HU.5, and 12 Westland Gazelle HT.3

SAM squadrons
  2 with British Aerospace Bloodhound 2 SAM

Queen's Flight
  1 with 3 British Aerospace Andover and 2 Westland Wessex

Missiles
  AIM-7 Sparrow III AAM
  AIM-9 Sidewinder AAM
  British Aerospace Red Top AAM
  British Aerospace Firestreak AAM
  British Aerospace Sky Flash AAM
  Aérospatiale AS.12 ASM
  Aérospatiale AS.30 ASM
  Matra/British Aerospace Martel ASM

  (24 British Aerospace Harrier GR.3)*
  (78 Panavia Tornado [out of a requirement for 220 FGA and 165 AD planned])
  (11 British Aerospace Nimrod AEW.3)
  (84 British Aerospace Hawk T.1)
  (9 British Aerospace VC10 K.1)
  (33 Boeing CH-47D Chinook)
  (7 Westland Puma)
  (AIM-9L Sidewinder AAM)
  (British Aerospace Sky Flash AAM)

Royal Air Force Regiment
  4 wing HQs
  6 field squadrons
  6 air defence squadrons with Rapier SAM
(Scorpion light tanks)
(Spartan APCs)

* Equipment within brackets is on order.

Avro Shackleton

Type: maritime reconnaissance and anti-submarine aircraft, and airborne early-warning aircraft
Crew: ten
Wings: metal cantilever mid-wing monoplane
Fuselage: metal semi-monocoque
Tail unit: metal cantilever
Landing gear: hydraulically actuated retractable tricycle unit
Powerplant: four Rolls-Royce Griffon 57 inline engines, each rated at 2,455 hp and driving two three-blade metal contra-rotating propellers, plus two Rolls-Royce

Viper 203 turbojets, each rated at 2,500-lb (1,134-kg) static thrust
Fuel capacity: 4,248 gallons (19,311 litres)
Avionics: comprehensive communication and navigation/attack equipment, including APS-20 long-range surveillance radar in AEW models
Armament: two 20-mm Hispano cannon, plus up to 10,000 lb (4,536 kg) of bombs, depth charges, mines or torpedoes
Dimensions: Span 119 ft 10 in (36.53 m)
Length 92 ft 6 in (28.19 m)
Height 23 ft 4 in (7.11 m)
Wing area: 1,458 ft² (135.45 m²)
Weights: Empty 57,800 lb (26,218 kg)
Loaded

Maximum 100,000 lb (45,360 kg)
Performance: speed 302 mph (486 kph); cruising speed 253 mph (407 kph); climb 850 ft (260 m) per minute at sea level; service ceiling 19,200 ft (5,852 m); range 4,215 miles (6,780 km)
Used also by: South Africa
Notes: The design of the Shackleton can be traced back to the Lancaster bomber of World War II, though the prototype first flew in 1949. The MR.1 entered service in 1950, and the maritime version is now used only by South Africa, British aircraft having been converted into AEW.2 models. The technical specification applies to the MR.3.

British Aerospace (BAC) Lightning

Type: all-weather interceptor fighter
Crew: one
Wings: metal cantilever high mid-wing monoplane
Fuselage: metal semi-monocoque
Tail unit: metal cantilever
Landing gear: hydraulically actuated retractable tricycle unit
Powerplant: two Rolls-Royce Avon 301 turbojets, each rated at 16,360-lb (7,421-kg) static thrust with afterburning
Fuel capacity:
Avionics: comprehensive communication and navigation/attack equipment
Armament: two Red Top or Firestreak air-to-air missiles, plus two optional 30-mm Aden cannon. Export models have provision for 6,000 lb (2,722 kg) of external stores above and below the wings
Dimensions: Span 34 ft 10 in (10.6 m)
Length 53 ft 3 in (16.25 m)
Height 19 ft 7 in (5.95 m)
Wing area: 460 ft² (42.74 m²)
Weights: Empty about 28,000 lb (12,700 kg)
Loaded
Maximum about 50,000 lb (22,680 kg)
Performance: speed 1,500 mph (2,415 kph) or Mach 2.27 at 40,000 ft (12,192 m); cruising speed 595 mph (958 kph); climb 50,000 ft (15,240 m) per minute at sea level; service ceiling over 60,000 ft (18,290 m); range 800 miles (1,290 km) with ventral tanks but no overwing tanks
Used also by: Saudi Arabia

Notes: The Lightning was Britain's first truly supersonic fighter, and resulted from the development of the English Electric P.1A research aircraft, which was redesigned to emerge as the P.1B fighter prototype in 1957. After much development work, this finally became the Lightning Mach 2 fighter, which entered RAF service in 1959. Since then there have been several variants:

1. Lightning F.1 initial production model with a relatively primitive afterburner, but Ferranti Airpass interception radar in the intake centrebody for the control of the two Firestreak missiles
2. Lightning F.2 with a fully variable

afterburner and improved all-weather capabilities
3. Lightning F.3 definitive interceptor model, with the Avon 301 series instead of the Avon 210 series, Red Top as well as Firestreak AAMs, a larger, flat-topped fin, and provision for two overwing ferry tanks
4. Lightning T.4 side-by-side operational trainer, based on the F.1A
5. Lightning T.5 side-by-side operational trainer, based on the F.3
6. Lightning F.6 development of the F.3, and at first known as the F.3A. The specification applies to this model.

British Aerospace (BAC) VC10

Type: long-range strategic transport aircraft
Crew: four, plus up to 150 passengers
Wings: metal cantilever low-wing monoplane
Fuselage: metal semi-monocoque
Tail unit: metal cantilever
Landing gear: hydraulically actuated retractable tricycle unit
Powerplant: four Rolls-Royce Conway 301 turbofans, each rated at 22,500-lb (10,206-kg) static thrust
Fuel capacity:
Avionics: comprehensive communication and navigation equipment
Armament: none
Dimensions: Span 146 ft 2 in (44.55 m)
Length 133 ft 8 in (40.74 m)
Height 40 ft (12.19 m)
Wing area: 2,932 ft² (272.4 m²)
Weights: Empty 146,000 lb (66,225 kg)
Loaded
Maximum 323,000 lb (146,512 kg)

Performance: speed 580 mph (933 kph) at 30,000 ft (9,144 m); cruising speed 518 mph (834 kph) at 38,000 ft (11,583 m); range 3,668 miles (5,903 km) with a payload of 59,000 lb (26,762 kg); range 5,370 miles (8,642 km) with a payload of 24,000 lb (10,886 kg)

Used also by: Oman
Notes: The RAF's VC10 C.1 is derived from the civil Standard VC10, with features from the Super VC10, such as uprated engines and extra fuel tankage in the fin. The first military VC10 flew in 1965.

British Aerospace (English Electric) Canberra

Type: light bomber, reconnaissance, intruder and general-purpose aircraft
Crew: two
Wings: metal cantilever mid-wing monoplane
Fuselage: metal semi-monocoque
Tail unit: metal cantilever
Landing gear: hydraulically actuated retractable tricycle unit
Powerplant: two Rolls-Royce Avon 206 turbojets, each rated at 11,250-lb (5,103-kg) static thrust
Fuel capacity:
Avionics: comprehensive communication and navigation equipment
Armament: none
Dimensions: Span 67 ft 10 in (20.68 m)
Length 66 ft 8 in (20.32 m)
Height 15 ft 7 in (4.75 m)

Wing area:
Weights: Empty
Loaded 49,000 lb (22,226 kg)
Maximum 55,000 lb (24,948 kg)
Performance: speed 560 mph (901 kph) at 40,000 ft (12,192 m); ceiling more than 60,000 ft (18,288 m); range 4,000 miles (6,440 km) with external fuel
Used also by: Argentina, Australia, Ecuador, Ethiopia, India, Peru, Rhodesia, South Africa, Venezuela
Notes: The English Electric Canberra has been the UK's most successful bomber since World War II. The prototype first flew in 1949, and the B.2 entered service in 1950. There have been several distinct models:
1. Canberra B.2, with 6,500-lb (2,948-kg) Avon 101 engines and a bomb load of 6,000 lb (2,722 kg)
2. Canberra PR.3, with more fuel in a longer fuselage

3. Canberra T.4 trainer with side-by-side controls
4. Canberra B.6 bomber, the updated B.2
5. Canberra PR.7 updated reconnaissance aircraft
6. Canberra B(I).8 intruder and interdiction aircraft, with 7,500-lb (3,402-kg) Avon 109 engines, four 20-mm cannon, 5,000 lb (2,268 kg) of bombs, and two AS.30 ASMs
7. Canberra PR.9 high-altitude reconnaissance aircraft, to which the specification above applies
8. Canberra T.11 and T.19 trainer versions of the B.2
9. Canberra B(I).12 interdiction aircraft. There were many other variants for bombing, reconnaissance, electronic warfare and the like. The most advanced models are the PR.9 and TT.17 used by the RAF for electronic reconnaissance.

British Aerospace (Hawker Siddeley Aviation) 125

Type: navigation trainer, light transport and utility aircraft
Crew: two to four, plus two pupils or up to eight passengers
Wings: metal cantilever low-wing monoplane
Fuselage: metal semi-monocoque
Tail unit: metal cantilever
Landing gear: hydraulically actuated retractable tricycle unit
Powerplant: two Rolls-Royce Bristol Viper Mark 520 turbojets, each rated at 3,310-lb (1,501-kg) static thrust
Fuel capacity: 1,018 gallons (4,628 litres) in integral wing tanks
Avionics: comprehensive communication and navigation equipment
Armament: none
Dimensions: Span 47 ft (14.33 m)
Length 47 ft 5 in (14.45 m)
Height 16 ft 6 in (5.03 m)

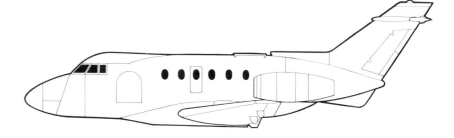

Wing area: 353 ft² (32.8 m²)
Weights: Empty
Loaded 20,500 lb (9,299 kg)
Maximum
Performance: (at normal take-off weight) maximum cruising speed 472 mph (760 kph) at 25,000 ft (7,620 m); climb to 25,000 ft (7,620 m) in 13 minutes; service ceiling 40,000 ft (12,200 m); range 1,338 miles (2,153 km)

Used also by: Brazil, Malaysia, Nicaragua, South Africa
Notes: Based on the Hawker Siddeley (de Havilland) 125 business jet, the HS 125 has appeared in three military versions:
1. Dominie T.1 advanced navigation trainer, based on the Series 2 aircraft
2. CC.1 communications aircraft, based on the Series 400 civil machine
3. CC.2 communications aircraft, based on the Series 600 civil machine.

British Aerospace (Hawker Siddeley Aviation) 748/Andover

Type: passenger and freight transport
Crew: three, plus up to 58 passengers
Wings: metal cantilever low-wing monoplane
Fuselage: metal semi-monocoque
Tail unit: metal cantilever
Landing gear: hydraulically actuated retractable tricycle unit
Powerplant: two Rolls-Royce Dart R.Da 7 Mk 535-2 turboprops, each rated at 2,280 ehp and driving a Dowty Rotol four-blade metal propeller
Fuel capacity: 1,440 gallons (6,550 litres) in two integral wing tanks
Avionics: comprehensive communication and navigation equipment
Armament: none
Dimensions: Span 98 ft 6 in (30.02 m)
Length 67 ft (20.42 m)
Height 24 ft 10 in (7.57 m)
Wing area: 810.75 ft² (75.35 m²)
Weights: Empty 25,453 lb (11,545 kg)

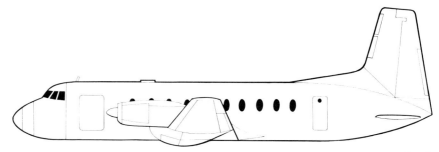

Loaded
Maximum 51,000 lb (23,133 kg)
Performance: cruising speed 281 mph (452 kph) for civil version at a weight of 38,000 lb (17,236 kg); climb 1,420 ft (433 m) per minute at sea level for civil version at a weight of 38,000 lb (17,236 kg); service ceiling 25,000 ft (7,620 m); combat radius with a load of 9,000 lb (4,082 kg) on a supply dropping mission 720 miles (1,158 km); range with a payload of 14,027 lb (6,363 kg) 1,474 miles (2,372 km)

Used also by: Australia, Belgium, Brazil, Brunei, Cameroon, Colombia, Ecuador, India, New Zealand, South Korea, Tanzania, Thailand, Upper Volta, Venezuela, Zambia
Notes: The HS 748 Military Transport is the military version of the Series 2A civil transport, with a large freight door and capable of a military overload. Maximum payload is 17,547 lb (7,959 kg). From 1979 production has been of the improved F. Series to B.

British Aerospace (Hawker Siddeley Aviation) Buccaneer

Type: strike and reconnaissance aircraft
Crew: two, seated in tandem
Wings: metal cantilever mid-wing monoplane
Fuselage: metal semi-monocoque
Tail unit: metal cantilever
Landing gear: hydraulically actuated retractable tricycle unit

Powerplant: two Rolls-Royce RB.168-1A Spey Mark 101 turbofans, each rated at 11,100-lb (5,035-kg) static thrust
Fuel capacity: 1,560 gallons (7,092 litres) in eight integral fuselage tanks, with the option of an extra 425 gallons (1,932 litres) in a bomb-door tank, plus provision for an auxiliary tank for 440 gallons (2,000 litres) in the bomb bay, and/or two 250- or 430-gallon (1,136- or 1,955-litre) underwing drop tanks
Avionics: comprehensive communication and navigation/attack equipment, including an air data system, a doppler radar navigation system, a search and fire-control radar incorporating a terrain warning system, and a strike sighting and computing system
Armament: four 1,000-lb (454-kg) Mark 10 bombs on the rotating bomb-bay door, plus four underwing pylons, each capable

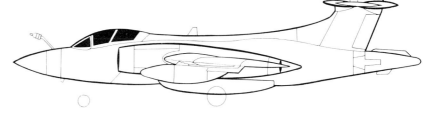

of carrying loads up to 3,000 lb (1,361-kg) in weight, for a total weapons load of 16,000 lb (7,257 kg). Typical underwing loads one each pylon are one or three 1,000-lb (454-kg) Mark N1 or Mark 10 bombs, two 500- or 540-lb (227- or 250-kg) bombs, six 500-lb (227-kg) bombs, one 18-tube 68-mm rocket pod, one 36-tube 2-in (51-mm) rocket pod, 3-in (76-mm) rockets, and one HSD/Matra Martel air-to-surface missile, up to a maximum of three missiles and one Martel systems pod. The bomb bay can also hold a reconnaissance pack
Dimensions: Span 44 ft (13.41 m)
Length 63 ft 5 in (19.33 m)
Height 16 ft 3 in (4.95 m)
Wing area: 514.7 ft² (47.82 m²)
Weights: Empty about 30,000 lb (13,608 kg)
Loaded 56,000 lb (25,400 kg)
Maximum 62,000 lb (28,123 kg)
Performance: speed 645 mph (1,038 kph) or Mach 0.85 at 200 ft (61 m); climb at

46,000-lb (20,865-kg) weight 7,000 ft (2,134 m) per minute at sea level; service ceiling more than 40,000 ft (9,144 m); combat radius with maximum weapons load 1,150 miles (1,850 km) on a hi-lo-hi strike mission
Used also by: South Africa
Notes: Designed by the Blackburn company in the late 1950s as an ultra-low level high-speed naval strike aircraft, the Buccaneer prototype first flew in 1958. Current models are:
1. S.2A for the RAF without Martel capability
2. S.2B for the RAF with Martel capability
3. S.2C for the Royal Navy without Martel capability
4. S.2D for the Royal Navy without Martel capability
5. S.50 for South Africa.

All S.2As are being brought up to S.2B standard.

British Aerospace (Hawker Siddeley Aviation) Harrier

Type: V/STOL close-support and reconnaissance aircraft
Crew: one
Wings: metal cantilever shoulder-wing monoplane
Fuselage: aluminium alloy and titanium semi-monocoque
Tail unit: metal cantilever
Landing gear: hydraulically actuated bicycle unit, with hydraulically actuated retractable wingtip-mounted outrigger wheels
Powerplant: one Rolls-Royce Bristol Pegasus Mark 103 vectored thrust turbofan, rated at 21,500-lb (9,752-kg) static thrust
Fuel capacity: 630 gallons (2,865 litres) in five fuselage and two wing integral tanks,

plus provision for two underwing 100-gallon (454-litre) combat drop tanks or two 330-gallon (1,500-litre) ferry tanks
Avionics: comprehensive communication and navigation/attack equipment, including Ferranti FE 541 inertial navigation and attack system (INAS), Smiths electronic head up display, Smiths air data computer, and Ferranti laser ranger and marked target seeker (LRMTS)
Armament: all armament is carried on five pylons, one under the fuselage and two under each wing, the fuselage and inner wing pylons being capable of carrying 2,000 lb (910 kg) of stores each, and the outer wing pylons 650 lb (295 kg) each, up to a current maximum of 5,000 lb (2,270 kg), though 8,000 lb (3,630 kg) can be carried. In addition, the strakes under the fuselage can each be replaced by a 30-mm Aden cannon pod. A typical load might con-

sist of two 30-mm cannon pods, one 1,000-lb (454-kg) bomb under the fuselage, two 1,000-lb (454-kg) bombs on the inner wing pylons, and two Matra 155 rocket pods, each with nineteen 68-mm SNEB rockets, on the outer pylons
Dimensions: Span 25 ft 3 in (7.7 m)
Length 45 ft 7¾ in (13.91 m)
Height 11 ft 3 in (3.43 m)
Wing area: 201.1 ft² (18.68 m²)
Weights: Empty 12,200 lb (5,533 kg)
Loaded
Maximum over 25,000 lb (11,340 kg)
Performance: speed 737 mph (1,186 kph) or Mach 0.972 at low level; dive speed Mach 1.3; climb (VTOL) 50,000 ft (15,240 m) per minute at sea level; service ceiling more than 50,000 ft (15,240 m); combat radius on a hi-lo-hi strike mission without drop tanks 260 miles (418 km); ferry range

2,070 miles (3,330 km); range with one inflight refuelling more than 3,455 miles (5,560 km)

Used also by: Spain, USA

Notes: The vectored-thrust Harrier prototype, the P.1127 Kestrel, first flew in 1960, and production aircraft entered service in 1969. There are several models:

1. Harrier GR.1, 1A and 3, single-seat close-support aircraft
2. Harrier T.2, 2A and 4, two-seat combat trainer with full combat capability, 55 ft 9½ in (17.0 m) in length, some 10 ft 3½ in (3.13 m) longer than single-seaters as a result of its extra forward fuselage section and tail boom
3. Sea Harrier FRS.1 single-seat fighter, reconnaissance and strike aircraft under development for the Royal Navy
4. Harrier Mark 50, or AV-8A single-seat close-support and tactical reconnaissance model for the US Marine Corps, whose aircraft are armed with a pair of AIM-9 Sidewinder air-to-air missiles
5. Harrier Mark 54, or TAV-8A two-seat operational trainer.

All RAF Harriers are retrofitted or are being retrofitted with laser rangefinders and marked target seekers in a 'chisel' nose.

British Aerospace (Hawker Siddeley Aviation) Hawk

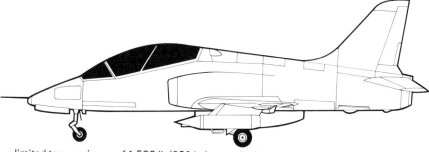

Type: trainer and close-support aircraft
Crew: two, seated in tandem
Wings: metal cantilever low-wing monoplane
Fuselage: metal semi-monocoque
Tail unit: metal cantilever
Landing gear: hydraulically actuated retractable tricycle unit
Powerplant: one Rolls-Royce/Turboméca RT.172-06-11 Adour 151 turbofan, rated at 5,340-lb (2,422-kg) static thrust
Fuel capacity: 365 gallons (1,659 litres) in integral wing and fuselage bag tanks, plus provision for one 100-gallon (454-litre) drop tank under each wing
Avionics: comprehensive communication and navigation equipment
Armament: (trainer) one 30-mm Aden cannon pod under the fuselage, plus one hardpoint under each wing, capable of carrying external stores of 1,000-lb (454-kg) weight, though normal training is limited to a maximum of 1,500 lb (680 kg); (close-support) one underfuselage and four underwing hardpoints, each capable of carrying 1,000 lb (454 kg) of external stores, up to a maximum weight of 5,660 lb (2,567 kg)
Dimensions: Span 30 ft 9¾ in (9.39 m)
Length 36 ft 7¾ in (11.17 m)
Height 13 ft 5 in (4.09 m)
Wing area: 179.6 ft² (16.69 m²)
Used also by: Finland, Indonesia, Kenya (?)
Notes: A useful and attractive little aircraft, the Hawk is capable of development into a number of other roles. The first two examples were delivered in 1976.
Weights: Empty 8,040 lb (3,647 kg)
Loaded 12,284 lb (5,572 kg)
Maximum 17,097 lb (7,755 kg)
Performance: speed 620 mph (997 kph); climb to 30,000 ft (9,145 m) in 6 minutes 6 seconds; service ceiling 48,000 ft (14,630 m); endurance as a trainer in 'clean' condition about 2 hours; ferry range with drop tanks 1,923 miles (3,095 km)

British Aerospace (Hawker Siddeley Aviation) Nimrod

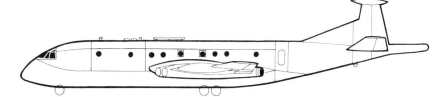

Type: maritime patrol aircraft
Crew: 12
Wings: metal cantilever low/mid-wing monoplane
Fuselage: metal semi-monocoque
Tail unit: metal cantilever
Landing gear: hydraulically actuated retractable tricycle unit
Powerplant: four Rolls-Royce RB.168-20 Spey Mark 250 turbofans, each rated at 12,140-lb (5,507-kg) static thrust
Fuel capacity: 10,730 gallons (48,780 litres) in fuselage, integral wing and wing leading-edge tanks, plus six optional tanks for a further 1,887.5 gallons (8,580 litres) in the weapons bay
Avionics: comprehensive communication and navigation/attack equipment, including a Marconi-Elliott navigation/attack system based on a Marconi-Elliott 920 ATC computer, EMI Searchwater long-range air-to-surface vessel search radar with a Ferranti FM 1600D digital computer controlling the inbuilt data processing subsystem, AQS 901 acoustics processing and display system operating with the aid of two Marconi-Elliott 920 ATC computers and a variety of active and passive sonobuoys, and Emerson Electronics ASQ-10A magnetic anomaly detector (avionics data are for MR.2)
Armament: a large weapons bay can accommodate up to nine torpedoes, or depth charges, mines or bombs in six lateral rows, plus two underwing hardpoints for the carriage of cannon pods, rocket pods, mines, or air-to-surface missiles, though this last capability is not currently available; sonobuoys are carried aft
Dimensions: Span 114 ft 10 in (35.0 m)
Length 126 ft 9 in (38.63 m)
Height 29 ft 8½ in (9.08 m)
Wing area: 2,121 ft² (197.0 m²)
Weights: Empty 92,000 lb (41,730 kg)
Loaded 177,500 lb (80,510 kg)
Maximum 192,000 lb (87,090 kg)
Performance: (MR.1) speed 575 mph (926 kph); cruising speed 547 mph (880 kph); patrol speed on two engines 230 mph (370 kph); service ceiling 42,000 ft (12,800 m); endurance 12 hours; ferry range 5,755 miles (9,265 km)
Used only by: UK
Notes: Derived from the same basic airframe as the Comet airliner, the Nimrod is an excellent maritime reconnaissance aircraft, with long range, high transit speed, good patrol endurance, advanced sensors and first-class weapons capability. There are four versions:

1. Nimrod MR.1 maritime reconnaissance variant, which is described in the technical section above, with the exception of the avionics subsection, which refers to the MR.2. In the MR.1, tactical navigation/attack is the task of an 8K Marconi-Elliott 920B digital computer
2. Nimrod R.1 electronic reconnaissance variant, which has no MAD tailboom and is thus only 118 ft (35.97 m) long
3. MR.2 maritime reconnaissance variant, basically the MR.1 refitted with more advanced sensor and navigation equipment, and new communications gear, for delivery during 1978–80
4. Nimrod AEW.3 airborne early warning variant, described separately.

British Aerospace (Hawker Siddeley Aviation) Nimrod AEW.3

Type: airborne early warning aircraft
Crew:
Wings: metal cantilever low/mid-wing monoplane
Fuselage: metal semi-monocoque
Tail unit: metal cantilever
Landing gear: hydraulically actuated retractable tricycle unit
Powerplant: four Rolls-Royce RB.168-20 Spey Mark 250 turbofans, each rated at 12,140-lb (5,507-kg) static thrust

Fuel capacity: probably in the order of 12,000 gallons (54,552 litres) in fuselage and wing tanks
Avionics: comprehensive communication and navigation equipment, plus Marconi-Elliott Avionics pulsed-doppler radar for ship and aircraft surveillance, with advanced automatic data processing
Armament: none
Dimensions: Span 115 ft 1 in (35.08 m)
Length 137 ft 5½ in (41.76 m)
Height 33 ft (10.06 m)
Wing area: 2.121 ft² (197.0 m²)
Weights: Empty
Loaded
Maximum
Performance: classified, but endurance is more than 10 hours
Used only by: UK
Notes: Derived from the Nimrod MR series, the Nimrod AEW.3 is an advanced early warning platform, suitable for operations at sea or over central Europe. The location of the two main radar scanners at each end of the fuselage rather than in a rotating radome offers a number of technical advantages, the benefits of which are enhanced by the excellent communications and tactical data systems. Electronic support measures (ESM) equipment is located in the fairings on top of the fin and on each wing leading edge.

British Aerospace (Hawker Siddeley Aviation) Sea Harrier

Type: carrierborne V/STOL fighter, strike and reconnaissance aircraft
Crew: one
Wings: metal cantilever shoulder-wing monoplane
Fuselage: metal semi-monocoque
Tail unit: metal cantilever
Landing gear: hydraulically actuated retractable bicycle unit, with stabilising outrigger wheels
Powerplant: one Rolls-Royce (Bristol) Pegasus 104 vectored-thrust turbofan, rated at 21,500-lb (9,752-kg) static thrust
Fuel capacity: 630 gallons (2,865 litres) in five integral fuselage and two integral wing tanks, plus provision for two 330-gallon (1,500-litre) ferry tanks, or two 100-gallon (455-litre) drop tanks

Avionics: comprehensive communication and navigation/attack equipment, including Ferranti Blue Fox multi-mode radar, Smiths head up display, and Decca doppler radar

Armament: two optional 30-mm Aden cannon under the fuselage, plus a variety of armament installations on one underfuselage and four underwing pylons, the three inner pylons being able to lift 2,000 lb (907 kg) each, and the outer pair 650 lb (295 kg) each, up to a maximum external load of 5,000 lb (2,270 kg), though 8,000 lb (3,630 lb) have been carried. The pylons can carry stores similar to those of the Harrier GR.3, with the addition of a pair of AIM-9 Sidewinder AAMs

Dimensions: Span 25 ft 3¼ in (7.7 m)
Length 47 ft 7 in (14.5 m)
Height 12 ft 2 in (3.71 m)

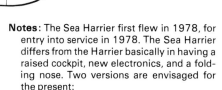

Wing area: 201.1 ft² (18.68 m²)
Weights: Empty 12,500 lb (5,670 kg)
Loaded
Maximum 25,000+ lb (11,340+ kg)
Performance: classified, but comparable with that of the Harrier GR.3
Used only by: UK

Notes: The Sea Harrier first flew in 1978, for entry into service in 1978. The Sea Harrier differs from the Harrier basically in having a raised cockpit, new electronics, and a folding nose. Two versions are envisaged for the present:
1. FRS. 1 combat aircraft, to which the specification above applies
2. T.4 two-seat trainer.

British Aerospace (Hawker Siddeley Aviation) Vulcan

Type: bomber and strategic reconnaissance aircraft
Crew: five
Wings: metal cantilever mid-wing delta monoplane
Fuselage: metal semi-monocoque
Tail unit: metal cantilever
Landing gear: hydraulically actuated retractable tricycle unit
Powerplant: four Rolls-Royce (Bristol Siddeley) Olympus 301 turbojets, each rated at 20,000-lb (9,072-kg) static thrust
Fuel capacity:
Avionics: comprehensive communication and navigation/attack equipment

Armament: up to 21,000 lb (9,526 kg) of conventional or nuclear bombs (bomber versions only)
Dimensions: Span 111 ft (33.83 m)
Length 105 ft 6 in (32.15 m)
Height 27 ft 2 in (8.26 m)
Wing area: 3,964 ft² (368.27 m²)
Weights: Empty
Loaded
Maximum about 250,000 lb (113,399 kg)
Performance: speed 640 mph (1,030 kph) or Mach 0.97 at high altitude; service ceiling about 65,000 ft (19,810 m); range about 4,600 miles (7,400 km)
Used only by: UK
Notes: The prototype Vulcan flew in 1952, and the bomber entered service in 1955, the second of the three British 'V' strategic

nuclear bombers of the 1950s. There are four variants:
1. Vulcan B.1 with 11,000-lb (4,990-kg) Olympus 101 turbojets, and inferior performance compared with later models. Later models were up-engined, eventually with 13,500-lb (6,124-kg) Olympus 104 engines
2. Vulcan B.1A with a bulged rear fuselage containing ECM equipment
3. Vulcan B.2, with a larger and thinner wing, the ability to carry the Blue Steel stand-off nuclear missile, and initially the 17,000-lb (7,711-kg) Olympus 201
4. Vulcan SR.2 strategic reconnaissance version, without armament but fitted with a variety of sensors.

British Aerospace (Scottish Aviation) Jetstream

Type: aircrew trainer and light transport aircraft

Crew: two, plus up to 12 passengers

Wings: aluminium alloy cantilever low-wing monoplane

Fuselage: aluminium alloy semi-monocoque

Tail unit: aluminium alloy cantilever

Landing gear: hydraulically actuated retractable tricycle unit

Powerplant: two Turboméca Astazou XVI D turboprops, each rated at 996 ehp and driving a Hamilton Standard three-blade metal propeller

Fuel capacity: 384 gallons (1,745 litres) in two integral wing tanks

Avionics: comprehensive communication and navigation equipment

Armament: none

Dimensions: Span 52 ft (15.85 m)
Length 47 ft 1½ in (14.37 m)
Height 17 ft 5½ in (5.32 m)

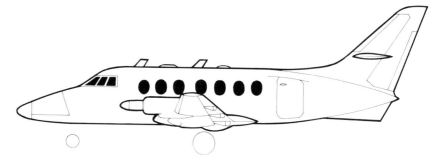

Wing area: 270 ft² (25.08 m²)

Weights: Empty 7,683 lb (3,485 kg)
Loaded
Maximum 12,566 lb (5,700 kg)

Performance: (at maximum take-off weight) speed 282 mph (454 kph) at 10,000 ft (3,050 m); cruising speed 269 mph (433 kph) at 15,000 ft (4,575 m); climb 2,500 ft (762 m) per minute at sea level; service ceiling 25,000 ft (7,620 m); range 1,380 miles (2,224 km)

Used only by: UK

Notes: Derived from the Handley Page HP 137 Jetstream, the Scottish Aviation machine appears in both civil and military guises, the two main military models being:

1. Jetstream T.1 for the RAF in the multi-engine pilot training scheme
2. Jetstream T.2 for the Royal Navy in the observer training programme, with MEL E 190 weather and terrain mapping radar in a 'thimble' nose.

British Aerospace (Scottish Aviation) SA-3-200 Bulldog Series 200

Type: flying and weapons training, and observation, liaison, reconnaissance and light strike aircraft

Crew: two, seated side-by-side

Wings: light alloy cantilever low-wing monoplane

Fuselage: light alloy semi-monocoque

Tail unit: light alloy cantilever

Landing gear: electro-mechanically actuated retractable tricycle unit

Powerplant: one Lycoming AEIO-360-A1B6 piston engine, rated at 200 hp and driving a Hartzell two-blade metal propeller

Fuel capacity: 32 gallons (145.5 litres) in four wing tanks

Avionics: communication and navigation equipment

Armament: provision for four underwing hardpoints, capable of accepting a maximum weapons load of 640 lb (290 kg), including light bombs, rockets, grenade launchers, and machine-gun pods

Dimensions: Span 33 ft 9 in (10.29 m)
Length 24 ft 11 in (7.59 m)
Height 8 ft 4 in (2.54 m)

Wing area:

Weights: Empty 1,810 lb (821 kg)
Loaded 2,304 lb (1,045 kg)
Maximum 2,601 lb (1,179 kg)

Performance: (at normal loaded weight) speed 173 mph (278 kph) at sea level; cruising speed 162 mph (260 kph) at 4,000 ft (1,220 m); climb 1,160 ft (353 m) per minute at sea level; service ceiling 18,500 ft (5,640 m); endurance 5 hours; range 621 miles (1,000 km)

Used only by: UK

Notes: Derived from the Series 120 Bulldog, the Series 200 has a retractable undercarriage, higher-mounted tailplane, better nose lines, an improved cockpit canopy, and improved performance and weights.

Handley Page Victor

Type: air-refuelling tanker and strategic reconnaissance aircraft

Crew: four or five

Wings: metal cantilever mid-wing monoplane

Fuselage: metal semi-monocoque

Tail unit: metal cantilever

Landing gear: hydraulically actuated retractable tricycle unit

Powerplant: four Rolls-Royce Conway 201 turbofans, each rated at 20,600-lb (9,344-kg) static thrust

Fuel capacity:

Avionics: comprehensive communication and navigation equipment, plus special reconnaissance gear in the SR.2

Armament: none

Dimensions: Span 120 ft (36.58 m)
Length 114 ft 11 in (35.05 m)
Height 30 ft 1½ in (9.2 m)

Wing area: 2,597 ft² (241.27 m²)

Weights: Empty 91,000 lb (41,277 kg)
Loaded
Maximum 233,000 lb (101,150 kg)

Performance: speed about 640 mph (1,030 kph) or Mach 0.92 at 36,000 ft (10,973 m); service ceiling 60,000 ft (18,290 m); range 4,600 miles (7,400 km)

Used only by: UK

Notes: The Victor was the third of the RAF's strategic nuclear bombers to enter service, the prototype having flown in 1952, and the initial production B.1 being taken into service in 1956. Their only defence is in ECM, which will not provide sufficient protection at high altitude in present conditions, so as the type cannot readily be converted to low-level penetration raids, the surviving aircraft have been converted into tankers and strategic reconnaissance aircraft.

Hawker Aircraft Hunter

Type: fighter, fighter-bomber and fighter-reconnaissance aircraft
Crew: one
Wings: metal cantilever mid-wing monoplane
Fuselage: metal semi-monocoque
Tail unit: metal cantilever
Landing gear: hydraulically actuated retractable tricycle unit
Powerplant: one Rolls-Royce Avon 207 turbojet, rated at 10,150-lb (4,604-kg) static thrust
Fuel capacity: 392 gallons (1,782 litres) internally
Avionics: comprehensive communication and navigation/attack equipment
Armament: four 30-mm Aden cannon with 150 rounds per gun, plus two 1,000-lb (454-kg) bombs and 24 3-in (76-mm) rockets under the wings, as well as two 230-gallon (1,046-litre) drop tanks
Dimensions: Span 33 ft 8 in (10.26 m)
Length 45 ft 10½ in (13.98 m)
Height 13 ft 2 in (4.26 m)
Wing area: 349 ft² (32.42 m²)
Weights: Empty 13,270 lb (6,020 kg)
Loaded 17,750 lb (8,051 kg)
Maximum 24,000 lb (10,885 kg)
Performance: speed 710 mph (1,144 kph) at sea level; 620 mph (978 kph) or Mach 0.94 at 36,000 ft (10,973 m); climb about 8,000 ft (2,438 m) per minute at sea level; climb 7 minutes 30 seconds to 45,000 ft (13,706 m); service ceiling 50,000 ft (15,240 m); range 1,840 miles 2,965 km) with maximum fuel; combat radius 219 miles (352 km) with 2,000 lb (907 kg) of bombs and drop tanks
Used also by: Chile, India, Iraq, Kenya, Kuwait, Lebanon, Peru, Qatar, Rhodesia, Singapore, Switzerland, Uruguay
Notes: The Hunter is the most successful fighter built in the UK since World War II, the prototype flying in 1951 and the F.1 entering service in 1953. Since that time the Hunter has been produced in a great number of versions for domestic and foreign use, and the type is still widely used as a ground-attack aircraft. The specification above applies to the FGA.9 ground-attack fighter.

Lockheed-Georgia C-130 Hercules

Type: tactical transport aircraft
Crew: four, plus up to 92 passengers
Wings: metal cantilever high-wing monoplane
Fuselage: aluminium and magnesium alloy semi-monocoque
Tail unit: metal cantilever
Landing gear: hydraulically actuated retractable tricycle unit
Powerplant: four Allison T56-A-15 turboprops, each rated at 4,508 ehp and driving a Hamilton Standard four-blade metal propeller, plus provision for eight Aerojet-General 15KS-1,000 JATO units, each rated at 1,000-lb (454-kg) static thrust for 15 seconds
Fuel capacity: 5,795 gallons (26,344 litres) in six integral wing tanks, and 2,264 gallons (10,292 litres) in two underwing pylon tanks
Avionics: comprehensive communication and navigation equipment
Armament: none
Dimensions: Span 132 ft 7 in (40.41 m)
Length 97 ft 9 in (29.78 m)
Height 38 ft 3 in (11.66 m)
Wing area: 1,745 ft² (162.12 m²)
Weights: Empty 75,331 lb (34,169 kg)
Loaded 155,000 lb (70,310 kg)
Maximum 175,000 lb (79,380 kg)
Performance: (at maximum take-off weight) cruising speed 386 mph (621 kph); economical cruising speed 345 mph (556 kph); climb 1,900 ft (579 m) per minute at sea level; service ceiling at a weight of 130,000 lb (58,970 kg) 33,000 ft (10,060 m); range with maximum payload 2,487 miles (4,002 km); range with maximum fuel and a payload of 20,000 lb (9,070 kg) 5,135 miles (8,264 km)
Used also by: many nations
Notes: Designed to a US Air Force requirement of 1951 for a tactical transport, the prototype Hercules first flew in 1954. The type has proved most successful and versatile, and there are numerous variants:

1. C-130A initial production aircraft for the USAF, with 3,750-shp T56-A-1A engines. There were several sub-variants, including the AC-130A gunship and GC-130A drone launcher
2. C-130B, with 4,050-shp T56-A-7A engines, different propellers and greater weights. Sub-variants include the WC-130B weather reconnaissance model and JC-130B air-snatch satellite recovery aircraft
3. C-130E, with more fuel capacity to increase range. Sub-variants include the DC-130E drone director, HC-130E for the Aerospace Rescue and Recovery Service, and WC-130E weather reconnaissance aircraft
4. C-130H, to which the technical specification above applies, with more powerful engines.

Among the prefixes indicating the C-130's functions are DC (drone director), EC (electronics, communications and ECM), HC (search and rescue, helicopter fuelling and spacecraft retrieval), KC (assault transport and probe-drogue refueller), LC (wheel/ski undercarriage) and WC (weather reconnaissance). The AC-130H is a gunship with the formidable armament of one 105-mm howitzer, one 40-mm cannon, two 20-mm or T-171 cannon, two 7.62-mm Miniguns and other optional weapons. The maximum payload of the C-130H is 43,811 lb (19,872 kg).

McDonnell Douglas (McDonnell Aircraft) F-4 Phantom II

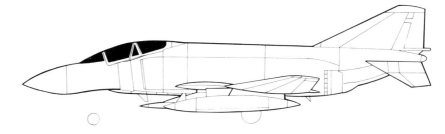

Type: all-weather multi-role fighter
Crew: two, seated in tandem
Wings: metal cantilever low-wing monoplane
Fuselage: metal semi-monocoque
Tail unit: metal cantilever
Landing gear: hydraulically actuated retractable tricycle unit
Powerplant: two General Electric J79-GE-17A turbojets, each rated at 17,900-lb (8,119-kg) static thrust with afterburning
Fuel capacity: 1,545 gallons (7,022 litres) in seven fuselage and two integral wing tanks, plus provision for one 500-gallon (2,270-litre) auxiliary tanks under the fuselage, and two 308-gallon (1,400-litre) tanks under the wings
Avionics: comprehensive communication and navigation/attack equipment, including a CPK-92A/A24G-34 central air data computer, AN/AJB-7 bombing system, AN/ASQ-91 (MOD) weapons release system, AN/ASG-26 (MOD) lead-computing optical sight; AN/ASA-32 automatic fire-control system, AN/APQ-120 fire-control system radar and AN/ARQ-77 AGM-12 control system
Armament: one M61A-1 20-mm multi-barrel cannon, four AIM-7 Sparrow air-to-air missiles semi-recessed under the fuselage, four AIM-9 Sidewinder or two Sparrow air-to-air missiles on two underwing pylons (Falcon, Shrike, Walleye and Bullpup missiles can also be carried on these stations); alternatively, the seven attachment points under the fuselage and wings can carry loads of up to 16,000 lb (7,250 kg) in weight: B-28, 43, 57 and 61 nuclear bombs; BLU-1, 27, 52, and 76 fire bombs; M117, M118, M129, MC-1, Mark 36, 81, 82, 83 and 84 bombs; gun pods; cluster bombs; ECM pods; rocket pods; and other stores.
Dimensions: Span 38 ft 7½ in (11.77 m)
Length 63 ft (19.2 m)
Height 16 ft 5½ in (5.02 m)
Wing area: 530 ft² (49.2 m²)
Weights: Empty 30,328 lb (13,757 kg)
Loaded 41,487 lb (18,818 kg)
Maximum 61,795 lb (28,030 kg)
Performance: (at maximum take-off weight) speed 1,500 mph (2,414 kph) or Mach 2.27 at high altitude with Sparrow missiles

only; speed 920 mph (1,464 kph) or Mach 1.19 at low altitude with Sparrow missiles only; cruising speed 571 mph (919 kph); climb 6,170 ft (1,881 m) per minute at sea level; service ceiling 28,100 ft (8,565 m); service ceiling with Sparrow missiles only more than 60,000 ft (19,685 m); combat radius on interdiction mission 712 miles (1,145 km); ferry range 1,978 miles (3,184 km)

Used also by: Greece, Iran, Israel, Japan, South Korea, Spain, Turkey, USA, West Germany

Notes: Probably the greatest fighter of the post-World War II era, the F-4 originated in a US Navy requirement of 1954 for a long-range all-weather attack fighter. The prototype flew in 1958, and the type began to enter service in 1960, being adopted by the USAF in addition to the US Navy. There have been numerous variants, including:

1. F-4A, with J79-GE-2 engines for the US Navy
2. F-2B, with J79-GE-8 engines, for the US Navy and Marine Corps as an all-weather fighter
3. RF-4B USMC reconnaissance version of the F-4B with multiple sensors
4. F-4C, with J79-GE-15 engines, a version of the F-4B for the USAF and Spain
5. F-4C Wild Weasel defence suppression aircraft for the USAF with ECM warning equipment, jamming pods, chaff dispensers and radiation-homing missiles
6. RF-4C multi-sensor reconnaissance version of the F-4C for the USAF
7. F-4D, with J79-GE-15 engines, a version of the F-4C with improved electronics for the USAF, Iran and South Korea
8. F-4E, to which the above technical specifications apply, a multi-role

fighter for air superiority, close support and interdiction missions, with an inbuilt cannon, improved electronics and advanced engines for the USAF, Greece, Iran, Australia, Israel, West Germany, Turkey and South Korea
9. F-4EJ version of the F-4E for Japan
10. RF-4E multi-sensor reconnaissance model of the F-4E for West Germany, Greece, Iran, Israel, Japan and Turkey
11. F-4F two-seat fighter with improved aerodynamics to increase manoeuvrability, and more advanced electronics, for West Germany
12. F-4G, a limited-production version of the F-4B with data link communications for the US Navy
13. F-4G Wild Weasel version of the F-4E, with special equipment for the suppression of enemy radar guidance systems
14. F-4J, with J79-GE-10 engines, as a development of the F-4B for the US Navy and Marine Corps, with a primary role of interception but with secondary ground-attack capability by virtue of its Westinghouse AN/AWG-10 pulse-doppler fire-control system, and Lear Siegler AJB-7 bombing system
15. F-4K version of the F-4B for the Royal Navy, with the electronics of the F-4J and a powerplant of two Rolls-Royce Spey RB.168-25R Mark 201 turbofans, each rated at 21,250-lb (9,639-kg) static thrust with afterburning
16. F-4M version of the F-4K for the Royal Air Force
17. F-4N, designation of updated F-4Bs
18. F-4S, designation for updated F-4Js with modified J79-GE-10B engines and improved AN/AWG-10A weapons control system.

Panavia Aircraft Tornado

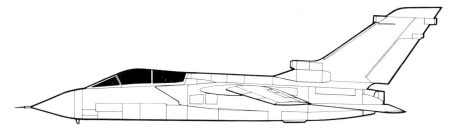

Type: multi-role combat aircraft
Crew: two, in tandem
Wings: variable-geometry metal cantilever shoulder-mounted monoplane
Fuselage: metal semi-monocoque
Tail unit: metal cantilever
Landing gear: hydraulically actuated retractable tricycle unit
Powerplant: two Turbo-Union RB.199-34R-4 turbofans, each rated at 16,000-lb (7,258-kg) static thrust with afterburning
Fuel capacity: internal self-sealing fuel tanks in the fuselage and wings, plus provision for underwing auxiliary fuel tanks
Avionics: comprehensive communications and navigation equipment; the primary attack/navigation system comprises a Texas Instruments multi-mode forward-looking radar (Marconi-Elliott multi-mode airborne interception radar in RAF air defence model), Ferranti 3-axis digital inertial navigation system, Decca Type 72 doppler radar, Microtecnica air data computer, Litef Spirit 3 16-bit central digital computer, Aeritalia radio-radar altimeter, Smiths/Teldix/OMI head up display, Ferranti nose-mounted laser rangefinder and marked-target receiver, Marconi-Elliott TV tabular display, Astronautics bearing distance heading indicator and contour map display, Siemens or Cossor SSR-3100 IFF transponder, Elettronica warning radar, and MSDS/Plessey/Decca passive ECM system
Armament: two 27-mm IWKA-Mauser cannon, and a variety of non-nuclear stores on three underfuselage hardpoints and four underwing hardpoints. The hardpoints can carry Sidewinder, Sky Flash, Sparrow and *Aspide* 1A air-to-air missiles; AS.30, Martel, *Kormoran* and Jumbo air-to-surface missiles; napalm tanks; BL-755 600-lb (272-kg) cluster bombs; Mk 83 or other 1,000-lb (454-kg) bombs; 'smart' and retarded bombs; Lepus flare bombs; reconnaissance pods; and active or passive ECM pods. The maximum external load is more than 15,000 lb (6,804 kg)
Dimensions: Span (spread) 45 ft 7¼ in (13.9 m); Span (swept) 28 ft 2½ in (8.6 m)
Length 54 ft 9½ in (16.7 m)
Height 18 ft 8½ in (5.7 m)
Wing area:
Weights: Empty 22,000–23,000 lb (9,980–10,430 kg)
Loaded 38,000–40,000 lb
Maximum 52,000 lb (23,587 kg)
Performance: speed about 1,450 mph (2,335 kph) or Mach 2.2 at 36,090 ft (11,000 m); speed about 910 mph (1,465 kph) or Mach 1.2 at low altitude; service ceiling over 50,000 ft (15,240 m); range about 1,000 miles (1,610 km) at high altitude with wings spread and on internal fuel; ferry range more than 3,000 miles (4.830 km) with external auxiliary tanks
Used also by: Italy, West Germany
Notes: Design of the 3-nation Tornado was completed in 1972, and the first prototype flew in 1974. First service deliveries should take place during 1979. The basic design had to fulfil six operational requirements:

1. close air support and battlefield interdiction
2. interdiction and counter-air strike
3. air superiority
4. interception
5. naval strike
6. reconnaissance.

There is also to be a trainer variant. The details given above are for the basic interdiction and strike model.

Société Européenne de Production de l'Avion ECAT (SEPECAT) Jaguar

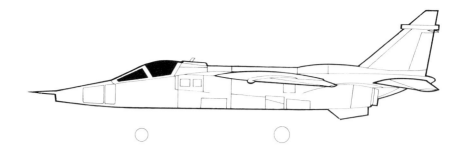

Type: strike fighter and trainer

Crew: one or two, in tandem

Wings: metal cantilever shoulder-wing monoplane

Fuselage: metal semi-monocoque

Tail unit: metal cantilever

Landing gear: hydraulically actuated retractable tricycle unit

Powerplant: two Rolls-Royce/Turboméca Adour 102 turbofans, each rated at 7,385-lb (3,350-kg) static thrust with afterburning

Fuel capacity: 924 gallons (4,200 litres) in four fuselage and two wings tanks, plus provision for three 264-gallon (1,200-litre) drop tanks, one under the fuselage and two under the wings

Avionics: comprehensive communication and navigation/attack equipment, including in the British versions Marconi-Elliott digital/inertial navigation and weapon aiming subsystem with an MCS 920M digital computer, E3R 3-gyro inertial platform, inertial velocity sensor, navigation control unit and projected map display; Marconi-Elliott air data computer; Smiths electronic head up display; Smiths FS6 horizontal situation indicator; Sperry C2J gyro amplifier master unit, compass controller and magnetic detector; Plessey weapon control system; and in the Jaguar S a Ferranti laser rangefinder and marked target seeker

Armament: (Jaguar A and S) two 30-mm cannon (DEFA 553 in Jaguar A, Aden in Jaguar S), plus five external hardpoints (one under the fuselage and two under each wing, the fuselage and inner wing points stressed to take loads of up to 2,205 lb (1,000 kg), and the outer wing points up to 1,102 lb (500 kg), to a maximum of 10,000 lb (4,535 kg) carried externally. The hardpoints can carry nuclear weapons, bombs, reconnaissance pods, missiles, rockets and fuel tanks

Dimensions: Span 28 ft 6 in (8.69 m)
Length 55 ft 2½ in (16.83 m)
Height 16 ft 0½ in (4.89 m)

Wing area: 258.33 ft² (24.0 m²)

Weights: Empty 15,432 lb (7,000 kg)
Loaded 24,000 lb (11,000 kg)
Maximum 34,000 lb (15,500 kg)

Performance: speed 990 mph (1,593 kph) or Mach 1.5 at 36,000 ft (11,000 m); speed 840 mph (1,350 kph) or Mach 1.1 at sea level; attack radius on internal fuel 507 miles (815 km) on a hi-lo-hi raid, 357 miles (575 km) on a lo-lo-lo raid; attack radius with external fuel tanks 818 miles (1,315 km) on a hi-lo-hi raid, 518 miles (835 km) on a lo-lo-lo raid; ferry range 2,614 miles (4,210 km) with maximum external fuel

Used also by: Ecuador, France, India, Oman

Notes: Evolved from the Breguet Br121, the Jaguar resulted from a British Aircraft Corporation and Breguet Aviation liaison to meet similar French and British air force requirements for an advanced trainer and attack aircraft. There are the following versions:

1. Jaguar A is a French single-seat tactical support aircraft
2. Jaguar B (Jaguar T.2) is a British two-seat operational trainer, with one 30-mm Aden cannon and a length of 53 ft 10½ in (16.42 m)
3. Jaguar E is a French two-seat advanced trainer, with two 30-mm DEFA 553 cannon and a length of 53 ft 10½ in (16.42 m)
4. Jaguar S (Jaguar GR.1) is a British single-seat tactical support model, similar to the Jaguar A but with superior navigation/attack systems
5. Jaguar International is the export version, based on the Jaguar S with more powerful Adour RT.172-26 engines, rated at 8,600-lb (3,900-kg) static thrust each with afterburning. There are various armament options, including a pair of overwing pylons for dogfighting missiles such as the Magic.

Société Nationale Industrielle Aérospatiale/Westland SA 330 Puma

Type: medium transport helicopter

Crew: two, plus accommodation for up to 20

Rotor: metal, carbon fibre and fibreglass cantilever four-blade main rotor; five-blade tail rotor

Fuselage: metal semi-monocoque

Landing gear: hydraulically actuated semi-retractable tricycle unit

Powerplant: two Turboméca Turmo IVC turboshafts, each rated at 1,575 shp

Fuel capacity: $339\frac{1}{2}$ gallons (1,544 litres) in flexible fuselage tanks, plus an optional 418 gallons (1,900 litres) in fuselage ferry tanks, and 154 gallons (700 litres) in external tanks

Avionics: full flight and navigation radar and computer, plus comprehensive radio

Armament: very varied, and including 20-mm cannon, 7.62-mm machine-guns, and a number of missile and rocket combinations

Dimensions: Span 49 ft $2\frac{1}{2}$ in (15.0 m)
Length (fuselage) 46 ft $1\frac{1}{2}$ in (14.06 m)
Height 16 ft $10\frac{1}{2}$ in (5.14 m)

Rotor disc area: 1,905 ft² (177.0 m²)

Weights: Empty (SA 330L) 7,915 lb (3,590 kg)
Loaded
Maximum 16,315 lb (7,400 kg)

Performance: (at 13,230 lb/6,000 kg AUW) speed 182 mph (294 kph); cruising speed 168 mph (271 kph); climb 1,810 ft (552 m) per minute at sea level; service ceiling 19,680 ft (6,000 m); range 355 miles (572 km) at cruising speed

Used also by: Algeria, Cameroon, Chad, Chile, Ecuador, Egypt, Ethiopia, Gabon, Indonesia, Iraq, Ivory Coast, Kenya, Kuwait, Morocco, Nepal, Nigeria, Pakistan, Portugal, South Africa, Spain, Sudan, Togo, Tunisia, Zaire

Notes: The SA 330 was developed to a French Army requirement, and adopted in 1967 by the RAF. The SA 330L is the current military model.

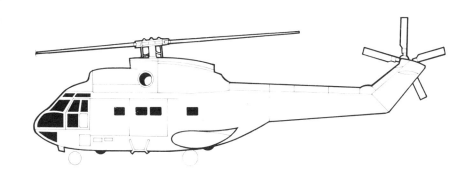

Société Nationale Industrielle Aérospatiale/Westland SA341/342 Gazelle

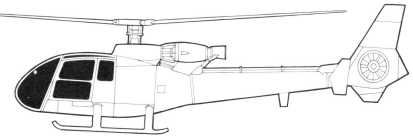

Type: light utility helicopter

Crew: one or two, plus three passengers

Rotor: plastic and glassfibre three-blade main rotor; 13-blade shrouded fan tail rotor

Fuselage: welded metal frame and metal semi-monocoque

Landing gear: twin steel tube skids

Powerplant: (SA 341) one Turboméca Astazou IIIA turboshaft, rated at 590 shp

Fuel capacity: 161 gallons (735 litres) in main, auxiliary and ferry tanks

Avionics: navigation and communication equipment

Armament: loads that can be carried include two 36-mm rocket pods, four AS.11 or HOT wire-guided missiles, two AS.12 missiles, four TOW missiles, two forward-firing 7.62-mm machine-guns, plus cabin- or chin-mounted 7.62-mm machine-guns

Dimensions: Span 34 ft $5\frac{1}{2}$ in (10.5 m)
Length (fuselage) 31 ft $3\frac{1}{4}$ in (9.53 m)
Height 10 ft $2\frac{3}{4}$ in (3.15 m)

Rotor disc area: 931 ft² (86.5 m²)

Weights: Empty (SA 341H) 2,002 lb (908 kg)
Empty (SA 342) 2,105 lb (955 kg)
Maximum (SA 341H) 3,970 lb (1,800 kg)
Maximum (SA 342) 4,190 lb (1,900 kg)

Performance: (at maximum take-off weight) speed 193 mph (310 kph) at sea level; cruising speed 164 mph (264 kph) at sea level; climb 1,770 ft (540 m) per minute at sea level for SA 341; climb 2,010 ft (612 m) per minute at sea level for SA 342; service ceiling 16,400 ft (5,000 m) for SA 341; service ceiling 14,100 ft (4,300 m) for SA 342; range 469 miles (755 km) for SA 342 with maximum fuel at economical cruising speed (144 mph/233 kph)

Used also by: Egypt, France, Iraq, Kuwait, Malaysia, Qatar, Senegal, Yugoslavia

Notes: A joint Anglo-French helicopter resulting from a 1967 programme. There are 10 versions:
SA 341B for British Army (Gazelle AH.1)
SA 341C for Royal Navy (Gazelle HT.2)
SA 341D for RAF (Gazelle HT.3)
SA 341E project for RAF communications (Gazelle HCC.4)
SA 341F for French Army
SA 341G civil version
SA 341H military export version
SA 342J civil version of SA 342L
SA 342K military version with 870 shp Astazou XIVH
SA 342L military version with improved tail rotor.

Boeing Vertol CH-47 Chinook

Type: medium transport helicopter
Crew: two or three, plus up to 44 passengers
Rotors: two metal cantilever three-blade main rotors
Fuselage: metal semi-monocoque
Landing gear: fixed tricycle unit
Powerplant: two Lycoming T55-L-11C turboshafts, each rated at 3,750 shp but delivering 7,200 shp through the combined transmission
Fuel capacity: 910 gallons (4,137 litres) in tanks in the fuselage external pods, or 868 gallons (3,944 litres) if the Crashworthy Fuel System is fitted
Avionics: communications and navigation equipment
Armament: none
Dimensions: Span 60 ft (18.29 m) each
  Length (fuselage) 51 ft (15.54 m)
  Height 18 ft 7¾ in (5.68 m)
Rotor disc area: 5,655 ft² (523.3 m²) in all
Weights: Empty 21,464 lb (9,736 kg)
  Loaded 33,000 lb (14,968 kg)
  Maximum 46,000 lb (20,865 kg)
Performance: (at maximum take-off weight) speed 189 mph (304 kph) at sea level; cruising speed 158 mph (254 kph); climb 2,880 ft (878 m) per minute at sea level; service ceiling 15,000 ft (4,570 m); combat radius with 6,400-lb (2,903-kg) payload 115 miles (185 km); ferry range 1,331 miles (2,142 km)
Used also by: Argentina, Australia, Canada, Italy, Libya, Morocco, Nigeria, Philippines,

South Korea, Spain, Syria, USA
Notes: Design of this family of all-weather medium transport helicopters began in 1956, with the first flight being made in 1961. There have been three production variants:
  1. CH-47A, with 2,200-shp Lycoming T55-L-5 or 2,650-shp T55-L-7 turboshafts
  2. CH-47B, with 2,850-shp T55-L-7C turboshafts and improved rotors
  3. CH-47C, to which the specification above relates.
Maximum payload, carried externally, is 25,250 lb (11,453 kg).

Westland Aircraft Scout and Wasp

Type: multi-role helicopter
Crew: two, plus up to four passengers
Rotors: metal cantilever four-blade main rotor; metal cantilever two-blade tail rotor
Fuselage: metal tube structure and metal semi-monocoque tailboom
Landing gear: twin metal skids (Scout) or fixed quadricycle unit (Wasp)
Powerplant: one Rolls-Royce (Blackburn) Nimbus 102 turboshaft, rated at 685 shp (Scout), or one Rolls-Royce (Blackburn) Nimbus 503 turboshaft, rated at 710 shp (Wasp)
Fuel capacity: 155 gallons (705 litres)
Avionics: comprehensive communication and navigation equipment
Armament: flexible guns of up to 20-mm calibre, fixed machine-gun installations, rocket pods, or guided weapons such as the SS.11 ATGW (Scout); two Mark 44 A/S torpedoes (Wasp)
Dimensions: Span 32 ft 3 in (9.83 m)
  Length (fuselage) 30 ft 4 in (9.24 m)
  Height (rotors turning) 11 ft 8 in (3.56 m)
Rotor disc area: 816.9 ft² (75.89 m²)
Weights: Empty (S) 3,232 lb (1,465 kg); (W) 3,452 lb (1,566 kg)
  Loaded
  Maximum (S) 5,300 lb (2,405 kg); (W) 5,500 lb (2,495 kg)
Performance: (Scout) speed 131 mph (211 kph) at sea level; climb 1,670 ft (510 m) per minute at sea level; effective ceiling 13,400 ft (4,085 m); range with four passengers 315 miles (410 km)
Performance: (Wasp) speed 120 mph (193 kph) at sea level; climb 1,440 ft (439 m) per minute at sea level; effective ceiling

12,200 ft (3,720 m); range with four passengers 270 miles (435 km)
Used also by: Bahrain, Brazil, Netherlands, New Zealand, South Africa
Notes: The Scout and Wasp both stem from the Saunders-Roe P.531 light helicopter,

which first flew in 1958. The first AH.1 Scout for the British Army flew in 1961, and the first HAS.1 Wasp for the Royal Navy in 1962. The last machine to be delivered was a Wasp, in 1974.

Westland Aircraft Wessex

Type: multi-role helicopter
Crew: two or three, plus up to 16 passengers
Rotors: metal cantilever four-blade main rotor; metal cantilever four-blade tail rotor
Fuselage: metal semi-monocoque
Landing gear: fixed tailwheel unit
Powerplant: one Rolls-Royce Coupled Gnome 110/111 turboshaft, rated at 1,350 shp
Fuel capacity:
Avionics: comprehensive communication and navigation equipment
Armament: installations include flexible machine-guns and ASMs
Dimensions: Span 56 ft (17.07 m)
Length (fuselage) 48 ft 4½ in (14.74 m)
Height 16 ft 2 in (4.93 m)
Main rotor disc area: 2,463 ft² (228.82 m²)
Weights: Empty 8,304 lb (3,767 kg)
Loaded
Maximum 13,500 lb (6,120 kg)
Performance: speed 132 mph (212 kph) at sea level; cruising speed 121 mph (195 kph); climb 1,650 ft (503 m) per minute at sea level; service ceiling 14,000 ft (4,300 m); range 478 miles (769 km)
Used also by: Australia, Bangladesh
Notes: The Wessex is basically the Sikorsky S-58 built under licence in Britain, with a variety of turboshaft engines. The Royal Navy's HAS.1 and 3 have Rolls-Royce (Napier) Gazelles, the RAF's HC.2 (to which the technical specification above applies), the coupled Gnomes.

Westland Aircraft Whirlwind

Type: general-purpose helicopter
Crew: three, plus up to eight passengers
Rotors: metal cantilever three-blade main rotor; metal cantilever two-blade tail rotor
Fuselage: metal semi-monocoque
Landing gear: fixed quadricycle unit
Powerplant: one Bristol Siddeley Gnome H.1000 turboshaft, rated at 1,050 shp
Fuel capacity:
Avionics: communication and navigation equipment

Armament: provision for the installation of various weapons, such as machine-guns and air-to-surface missiles
Dimensions: Span 53 ft (16.15 m)
Length (fuselage) 44 ft 2 in (13.46 m)
Height 15 ft 7½ in (4.76 m)
Rotor disc area: 2,206 ft² (204.96 m²)
Weights: Empty 4,694 lb (2,129 kg)
Loaded 8,000 lb (3,629 kg)
Maximum
Performance: Speed 109 mph (175 kph); cruising speed 104 mph (167 kph); climb

1,200 ft (366 m) per minute at sea level at 58 mph (93 kph); hovering ceiling in ground effect 15,800 ft (4,816 m)
Used also by: Brazil, Nigeria, Qatar
Notes: The Westland Whirlwind is basically the Sikorsky S-55 built under licence in the UK, but extensively developed to produce the prolific HAR series for the RAF and Royal Navy. The HAR.10, to which the specification above applies, is the turboshaft-powered model which first flew in 1959. Maximum payload of the HAR.10 is 2,000 lb (907 kg).

Westland Helicopters Sea King

Type: anti-submarine helicopter, with secondary search and transport roles
Crew: four, and up to 22 passengers
Rotor: metal cantilever five-blade main rotor; metal cantilever six-blade tail rotor
Fuselage: light alloy stressed skin
Landing gear: hydraulically actuated retractable tailwheel unit
Powerplant: two Rolls-Royce Gnome H.1400-1 turboshafts, each rated at 1,660 shp
Fuel capacity: 800 gallons (3,636 litres) in fuselage bag tanks, plus provision for an internal auxiliary tank
Avionics: comprehensive communication and navigation/attack equipment, including a fully integrated all-weather hunter-killer weapons system, based on Plessey Type 195 dipping sonar, Bendix AN/AQS-13B Mark 50 dipping sonar, Marconi-Elliott AD 580 doppler navigation system, and AW 391 search radar
Armament: four Mark 44 homing torpedoes or four Mark 11 depth charges
Dimensions: Span 62 ft (18.9 m)
Length (fuselage) 55 ft 9¾ in (17.01 m)
Height 16 ft 10 in (5.13 m)
Rotor disc area: 3,019 ft² (280.5 m²)
Weights: Empty about 13,000 lb (5,896 kg)
Loaded
Maximum 21,000 lb (9,525 kg)
Performance: (at maximum take-off weight) speed 143 mph (230 kph); cruising speed 129 mph (208 kph) at sea level; climb 2,020 ft (616 m) per minute at sea level; service ceiling 10,000 ft (3,050 m); hovering ceiling in ground effect 5,000 ft (1,525 m); range with maximum load about 350 miles (563 km); range with maximum fuel 937 miles (1,507 km)
Used also by: Australia, Belgium, Brazil, Egypt, India, Libya, Norway, Pakistan, Saudi Arabia, West Germany
Notes: The Sea King is derived from the Sikorsky S-61 series, much altered by Westland. The type is capable of various missions (ASW, search and rescue, tactical troop transport, casualty evacuation, and freighting), and the following versions are in service:
1. Sea King HAS.1 ASW helicopter for the Royal Navy
2. Sea King HAS.2 ASW and SAR helicopter for the Royal Navy, with uprated engine

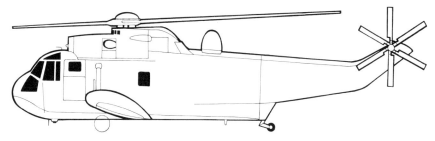

3. Sea King HAR.3 SAR helicopter for the RAF, with uprated engine
4. Sea King Mark 41 SAR helicopter for West Germany
5. Sea King Mark 42 ASW helicopter for the Indian Navy
6. Sea King Mark 43 SAR helicopter for the Royal Norwegian Air Force
7. Sea King Mark 45 ASW helicopter for the Pakistan Navy
8. Sea King Mark 47 ASW helicopter for the Egyptian Navy, ordered by Saudi Arabia
9. Sea King Mark 48 SAR helicopter for the Belgian Air Force
10. Sea King Mark 50 ASW helicopter for the Royal Australian Navy.

The technical details above refer to the HAS.2/HAR.3/Mark 50 series. Maximum payload is 6,500 lb (2,948 kg).

Westland Helicopters/Société Nationale Industrielle Aérospatiale Lynx

Type: multi-role military helicopter
Crew: one to four, plus up to 10 passengers
Rotor: steel and glassfibre cantilever four-blade main rotor; light alloy and glassfibre cantilever four-blade tail rotor
Fuselage: light alloy and glassfibre semi-monocoque
Landing gear: twin metal skids (general-purpose version) or fixed tricycle unit (naval version)
Powerplant: two Rolls-Royce BS.360-07-26 Gem turboshafts, each rated at 900 shp maximum contingency rating
Fuel capacity: 202 gallons (918 litres) in five fuselage bag tanks
Avionics: comprehensive communication and navigation/attack equipment, including Avimo-Ferranti 530 lightweight stabilised sight or other acquisition/guidance sights relevant to the weapons being carried
Armament: see breakdown in Notes below
Dimensions: Span 42 ft (12.802 m)
Length (overall) 49 ft 9 in (15.163 m)
Height 12 ft (3.66 m)
Rotor disc area: 1,385.4 ft² (128.7 m²)
Weights: Empty (general-purpose) 6,144 lb (2,787 kg)
Empty (ASW) 7,037 lb (3,192 kg)
Loaded 9,500 lb (4,309 kg)
Maximum 10,500 lb (4,763 kg)
Performance: (general-purpose version at normal loaded weight) speed 207 mph (333 kph); cruising speed 175 mph (282 kph); climb 2,180 ft (664 m) per minute at sea level; service ceiling more than 25,000 ft (7,600 m); endurance 3 hours 26 minutes; combat radius about 235 miles (378 km); ferry range 834 miles (1,342 km)
Performance: (naval version at normal loaded weight) speed 200 mph (322 kph); cruising speed 167 mph (269 kph); climb

2,020 ft (616 m) per minute at sea level; service ceiling more than 25,000 ft (7,600 m); endurance 3 hours 26 minutes; combat radius 209 miles (336 km); ferry range 650 miles (1,046 km)

Used also by: Argentina, Brazil, Denmark, Egypt, France, Netherlands and others

Notes: The Lynx, designed by Westland but built by Westland and Aérospatiale on a 70/30 basis, is one of the world's outstanding helicopters, being fast, easy to operate, very agile and capable of carrying loads of great weight. The main versions are currently:

1. Lynx AH.1 general-purpose and utility helicopter for the British Army, with tactical troop transport, logistic support, armed escort, anti-tank strike, casualty evacuation, reconnaissance, and search and rescue as its prime missions. Armament can comprise one 20-mm AME 621 cannon with 1,500 rounds, or one 7.62-mm GEC Minigun multi-barrel machine-gun in the cabin or with 3,000 rounds in an Emerson Minitat turret; plus one pylon on each side of the cabin, able to carry two Minigun pods, two rocket pods (of eighteen 68-mm or seven 2.75-in projectiles), or up to six BAC Hawkswing or Aérospatiale AS.11 air-to-surface missiles, or eight Aérospatiale/MBB HOT or Hughes TOW air-to-surface missiles (with six or eight reload rounds carried in the cabin)

2. Lynx HAS.2 anti-submarine helicopter for the Royal Navy. Armament can comprise two Mark 44 or 46 homing torpedoes or two Mark 11 depth charges, operated in conjunction with Alcatel DUAV 4 lightweight dunking sonar; for anti-shipping strike, the Lynx can carry four BAC CL834 Sea Skua, four AS.12 or similar air-to-surface missiles, in conjunction with Ferranti Seaspray search radar

3. Lynx (French Navy), similar to the HAS.2 but with more advanced target acquisition gear

4. Lynx HAR Mark 25/UH-14A for the Royal Netherlands Navy in the SAR and ASW roles respectively.

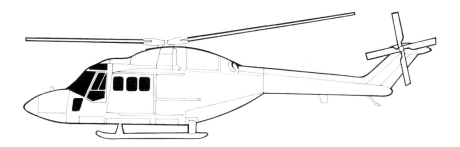

Aérospatiale AS.12

Type: air-to-surface tactical guided missile
Guidance: command to line-of-sight by means of twin wires
Dimensions: Span 25½ in (65.0 cm)
Body diameter 7 in (18.0 cm)
Warhead diameter 8¼ in (21.0 cm)
Length 6 ft 1⅜ in (1.87 m)
Booster: dual-thrust solid-propellant rocket
Sustainer: see above
Warhead: 62½ lb (28.4 kg) high explosive
Weights: Launch 170 lb (77 kg)
Burnt out
Performance: speed at impact 230 mph (370 kph); range 5 miles (8 km)
Used also by: Netherlands and other nations
Notes: Derived from the SS.12 battlefield missile, the AS.12 arms a number of maritime and military patrol aircraft. Of the same basic design and principle as the AS.11/SS.11, the AS.12/SS.12 carry a far greater punch by virtue of their larger warheads. The OP.3C warhead, for example, penetrates 1½ in (4.0 cm) of armour before exploding on the other side.

Aérospatiale AS.30

Type: air-to-surface tactical guided missile
Guidance: radio command
Dimensions: Span 39 $\frac{2}{8}$ in (1.0 m)
Body diameter 13$\frac{1}{2}$ in (34.2 cm)
Length (X12 warhead) 12 ft 7 in (3.84 m); (X35 warhead) 12 ft 9 in (3.885 m)
Booster: dual-thrust solid-propellant rocket
Sustainer: see above
Warhead: 507 lb (230 kg) high explosive
Weights: Launch 1,146 lb (520 kg)
Burnt out
Performance: speed Mach 1.3; range up to 7$\frac{1}{2}$ miles (12 km)
Used also by: India, Peru, South Africa, Switzerland, West Germany
Notes: Similar in design to the AS.20, the AS.30 is a much larger weapon, capable of carrying a more powerful warhead over longer ranges. There are two methods of guidance: optically, the operator in the aircraft steering the flares on the missile's tail onto the target, or automatically, with infra-red sensors on the aircraft providing information for computer control. A laser-guided version of the AS.30 is under development with the designation 'Ariel'.

British Aerospace Bloodhound Mark 2

Type: mobile surface-to-air tactical guided missile
Guidance: semi-active radar homing
Dimensions: Span 9 ft 3$\frac{1}{2}$ in (2.83 m)
Body diameter 21$\frac{1}{2}$ in (54.6 cm)
Length 27 ft 9 in (8.46 m)
Booster: four solid-propellant rockets
Sustainer: two Rolls-Royce (Bristol Siddeley) Thor ramjets
Warhead: high explosive
Weights: Launch 5,410 lb (2,454 kg)
Burnt out
Performance: range more than 50 miles (80 km); effective ceiling about 98,425 ft (30,000 m)
Used also by: Singapore, Sweden, Switzerland
Notes: Developed from the Bristol Aircraft Bloodhound Mark 1, the Mark 2 version of the weapon has improved capabilities in an ECM environment by virtue of having continuous-wave doppler radar instead of pulse radar. Once a target has been found by a surveillance radar, the Bloodhound site's Firelight (mobile) or Scorpion (static) target-illuminating radar (TIR) 'lights up' the target for the missile's seeker. The missile is then fired by the launch control post, which supervises the activities of a four-missile section.

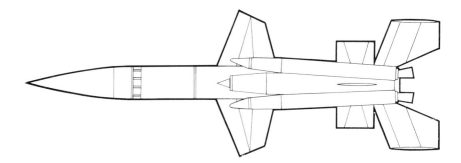

British Aerospace (BAC) Sea Skua

Type: helicopter-launched air-to-surface anti-shipping missile
Guidance: semi-active radar homing
Dimensions: Span 24$\frac{2}{5}$ in (62.0 cm)
Body diameter 8$\frac{3}{4}$ in (22.2 cm)
Length 9 ft 4$\frac{1}{8}$ in (2.85 cm)
Booster: dual-thrust solid-propellant rocket
Sustainer: see above
Warhead: 77-lb (35-kg) high explosive
Weights: Launch 325 lb (147 kg)
Burnt out

Performance: range 9 miles (14.5 km)
Used by: under development for UK
Notes: The Sea Skua is designed as an anti-shipping missile for the defence of frigates against missile-armed fast attack craft, and larger vessels as well. The target is illumined by the launch helicopter's Ferranti Seaspray radar, and the missile then homes automatically. The range of the missile will probably be great enough for the helicopter to be immune from the target's AA defences. Sea Skua is a wave-skimming missile.

British Aerospace (HSD) Firestreak

Type: air-to-air tactical guided missile
Guidance: infra-red homing
Dimensions: Span 29$\frac{1}{2}$ in (74.9 cm)
Body diameter 8$\frac{3}{4}$ in (22.225 cm)
Length 10 ft 5$\frac{1}{2}$ in (3.19 m)
Booster: dual-thrust solid-propellant rocket
Sustainer: as above
Warhead: about 50 lb (22.7 kg) high explosive
Weights: Launch about 300 lb (136 kg)
Burnt out
Performance: speed more than Mach 2; range between 0$\frac{3}{4}$ and 5 miles (1.2 and 5 km)
Used also by: Saudi Arabia
Notes: The Firestreak is a pursuit-course missile used on the Lightning fighter.

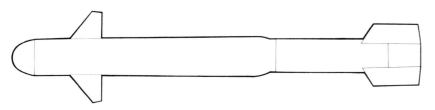

British Aerospace (HSD) Red Top

Type: air-to-air tactical guided missile
Guidance: infra-red homing
Dimensions: Span 35$\frac{3}{4}$ in (90.8 cm)
Body diameter 8$\frac{3}{4}$ in (22.225 cm)
Length 10 ft 10$\frac{3}{8}$ in (3.32 m)
Booster: dual-thrust solid-propellant rocket
Sustainer: as above
Warhead: 68 lb (31 kg) high explosive

Weights: Launch about 330 lb (150 kg)
Burnt out
Performance: speed about Mach 3; range at least 7$\frac{1}{2}$ miles (12 km)
Used also by: Saudi Arabia
Notes: Originally known as the Firestreak Mark IV, the Red Top maintains the basic design of the earlier missile, but is far more advanced electronically, has a larger warhead, and is powered by an improved motor. The Red Top can engage the target from virtually any direction.

British Aerospace (HSD) Sky Flash

Type: air-to-air tactical guided missile
Guidance: semi-active radar homing
Dimensions: Span 40 in (1.02 m)
    Body diameter 8 in (20.0 cm)
    Length 12 ft 1 in (3.68 m)
Booster: Aerojet General solid-propellant rocket
Sustainer: none
Warhead: 66 lb (30 kg) high explosive
Weights: Launch 425 lb (193 kg)
    Burnt out
Performance: speed more than Mach 2.25; range 31 miles
Used also by: Sweden
Notes: Based on the Raytheon AIM-7E Sparrow III, the Sky Flash uses a different guidance package specially designed by Marconi, and offering a very high hit probability with all-round attack capability.

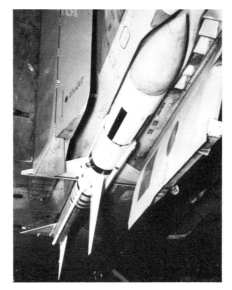

Matra/British Aerospace (HSD) AS.37/AJ.168 Martel

Type: air-to-surface tactical guided missile
Guidance: passive radar homing, or TV guidance
Dimensions: Span 3 ft 11¼ in (1.2 m)
    Body diameter 15¾ in (40.0 cm)
    Length (AS.37) 13 ft 6¼ in (4.12 m); (AJ.168) 12 ft 8½ in (3.87 m)
Booster: Hotchkiss-Brandt/SNPE Basile solid-propellant rocket
Sustainer: Aérospatiale/SNPE Cassandre solid-propellant rocket
Warhead: 331 lb (150 kg) high explosive
Weights: Launch (AS.37) 1,168 lb (530 kg); (AJ.168) 1,213 lb (550 kg)
    Burnt out
Performance: speed below Mach 1; range perhaps 37¼ miles (60 km) maximum, or 18½ miles (30 km) when launched at Mach 1 at low altitude
Used also by: France
Notes: There are two versions of the Martel (Missile Anti-Radar and TELevision):
1. AS.37 anti-radar version made by Matra, which homes onto radar antennae
2. AJ.168 TV-homing version made by British Aerospace, which is guided onto the target by the aircraft's weapons operator, who watches the image transmitted by the TV camera in the missile's nose.

Naval Weapons Center AIM-9 Sidewinder

Type: air-to-air tactical guided missile
Guidance: infra-red homing
Dimensions: Span 24⅘ in (63.0 cm)
    Body diameter 5 in (12.7 cm)
    Length 9 ft 4⅕ in (2.85 m)
Booster: Rocketdyne/Bermite Mark 36 Model 6 solid-propellant rocket
Sustainer: none
Warhead: WDU-17/B annular-blast high explosive with an active optical (laser) fuse
Weights: Launch 190 lb (86 kg)
    Burnt out
Performance: speed Mach 2.5; range 11 miles (17.7 km)
Used also by: many other nations
Notes: The AIM-9 Sidewinder has been a front-line weapon since the mid-1950s, and there are many versions of this still effective air-to-air guided missile:
1. AIM-9A prototype model, fired successfully fired in 1953
2. AIM-9B initial production model by Philco and General Electric, with a fin span of 22 in (56.0 cm), a length of 9 ft 3½ in (2.83 m), a weight of 159 lb (72 kg), and a motor made by the Naval Powder Plant. Speed is Mach 2 and ceiling more than 49,210 ft (15,000 m), but range is only 1,202 yards (1,100 m)
3. AIM-9C semi-active radar homing version of the AIM-9B
4. AIM-9D with Rocketdyne Mark 36 Model 5 motor to provide greater speed and range. Span is 25 in (64.0 cm), length 9 ft 6½ in (2.91 m), weight

185 lb (84 kg), and notable visual differences to earlier models are broader chord foreplanes, more swept tailplanes, and a tapering nose

5. AIM-9E improved AIM-9B, produced by Philco for the USAF with Thiokol Mark 17 motors
6. AIM-9G improved version of the AIM-9D with enhanced target acquisition, made by Raytheon for the USAF and USN

7. AIM-9H, based on the AIM-9G, with solid-state guidance, updated electronics to improve flexibility, and improved close-range dogfighting abilities for the USN
8. AIM-9J advanced model of the AIM-9E, with improved dogfighting capabilities given by revised foreplanes, and being made for the USAF by Ford Aerospace (successor to Philco)
9. AIM-9J-3 (or AIM-9J+) updating of

the AIM-9J with solid-state electronics
10. AIM-9L (Super Sidewinder), latest version for the USAF and USN, to which the technical specification above relates. This model is distinguishable from earlier Sidewinders by its double-delta foreplanes to improve manoeuvrability and hence dogfighting capabilities. The seeker head has also been improved, allowing aircraft fitted with the AIM-9L to attack from any angle.

Raytheon (Missile Systems Division) AIM-7 Sparrow III

Type: air-to-air tactical guided missile
Guidance: semi-active radar homing
Dimensions: Span 3 ft 4 in (1.02 m)
        Body diameter 8 in (20.3 cm)
        Length 12 ft (3.66 m)
Booster: Hercules Mark 58 Model O solid-propellant rocket
Sustainer: none
Warhead: 88 lb (40 kg) continuous-rod high explosive
Weights: Launch 500 lb (227 kg)
        Burnt out
Performance: speed more than Mach 3.5; range 31 miles (50 km)
Used also by: Belgium, Greece, Japan, Iran, Israel, Italy, Spain, USA, West Germany
Notes: The Sparrow is an all-weather all-altitude air-to-air missile of great power, and can also be used in the surface-to-surface, surface-to-air, and air-to-surface capacities. There are several versions of the Sparrow III:

1. AIM-7C initial production model, with an Aerojet General motor
2. AIM-7D improved model
3. AIM-7E, weighing 441 lb (200 kg). In its RIM-7H form, the AIM-7E is used in the NATO Sea Sparrow system
4. AIM-7F with a more powerful motor and warhead, plus greater manoeuvrability. The technical specification above relates to this model.

Illustration Credits   Picture Editor: Jonathan Moore

All artworks in this volume were produced by The County Studio, Leicestershire.

Unless otherwise indicated, all photographs were supplied through Military Archives and Research Services (MARS), London.

Key to picture positions: (T) = top, (C) = centre, (B) = bottom.

21) Chieftain main battle tank of B Sqdn, Queen's Royal Irish Hussars on exercise in the Polle area of West Germany; January 1973 (Crown Copyright (MOD-Army), London)
22(T) Scorpion light tank (Alvis Ltd., Warwickshire)
22(B) Saladin armoured car of the Queen's Own Hussars on patrol in Hong Kong; April 1966 (Crown Copyright (MOD-Army), London)
23) Ferret scout car of the Canadian Armed Forces; 1971 (Canadian Armed Forces, Ottawa)
24) Three FV432s of the 2nd Royal Irish Rangers awaiting orders to attack during Exercise Swordthrust; October 1975 (Crown Copyright (MOD-Army), London)
25) M110 8-in howitzers of the British Army during exercises in W. Germany; February 1973 (Crown Copyright (MOD-Army), London)
26(T) M107 175-mm self-propelled gun during firing trials at the Royal School of Artillery, Larkhill, Wiltshire; December 1973 (Crown Copyright (MOD-Army), London)
26(B) M109 self-propelled howitzer of the Bundeswehr (Federal German Army, Bonn)
27(T) Abbot self-propelled guns firing on Salisbury Plain; February 1978 (Crown Copyright (MOD-Army), London)
27(B) FH-70 155-mm gun-howitzer during British Army firing exercises at Larkhill, Wiltshire (Crown Copyright (MOD-Army), London)
28(T) 105-mm Light Gun being fired on Salisbury Plain by 13 Light Battery, RA; October 1975 (Crown Copyright (MOD-Army), London)
28(B) M-1956 105/14 howitzer (Canadian Armed Forces, Ottawa)
29(T) 40-mm towed light anti-aircraft gun M-1948 of the Finnish Army (Finnish Army, Helsinki)
29(B) Bofors M-1948 40-mm light anti-aircraft gun of the Norwegian Army (Norwegian Army Photo, Oslo)
30(T) Carl Gustav M2-550 84-mm recoilless rifle deployed ready for action. The loader kneels with a reload round ready (FFV Ordnance Div., Sweden)
30(C) Carl Gustav M2-550 recoilless rifle deployed ready for action (FFV Ordnance Div., Sweden)
30(B) Wombat anti-tank team from 'A' Company, 2 Parachute Regiment in NBC protective clothing fires practice rounds on the Sennelager Ranges, W. Germany; 1976 (Crown Copyright (MOD-Army), London)
31(T) Men of the 1st Bn. The Gordon Highlanders receive instructions on a Mobat anti-tank gun; October 1972 (Crown Copyright (MOD-Army), London)
31(B) Launch of a Rapier missile during trials at a Ministry of Defence range (British Aerospace, London)
32(T) Swingfire long-range anti-tank missile being launched from a Ferret scout car of the Parachute Squadron of the Royal Armoured Corps (British Aerospace, London)
32(C) TOW anti-tank missile in service with the Canadian Armed Forces; 1977 (Canadian Armed Forces, Ottawa)
32(B) TOW anti-tank missile mounted on a tracked APC of the US Army (Hughes Aircraft Co., California, USA)
33(T) *Milan* man-portable anti-tank guided missile, showing both the launch tube/container and sight (Euromissile, France)
33(B) Blowpipe is mainly a man-portable anti-aircraft missile and shoulder-fired launch tube. It is capable of dealing with lightly armoured vehicles and small surface craft and has been fitted in both ships and aircraft (Short Brothers Ltd., Belfast)
34(T) L1A1 81-mm light mortar being prepared for firing (Crown Copyright (MOD-Army), London)
34(B) Men of the Royal Regiment of Fusiliers at the ready with an L7 machine-gun during an exercise in West Germany; 1977 (Crown Copyright (MOD-Army), London)
35(T) Infantryman firing an L2A3 Sterling sub-machine gun during an exercise at Bassingbourn (Crown Copyright (MOD-Army), London)
35(B) L34A1 Sterling sub-machine gun (Sterling Armament Co. Ltd.)
36 L1A1 self-loading rifle (G. Cornish)
41(T) HMS *Resolution* (S22) nuclear-powered ballistic missile submarine. *Resolution* is fitted with 16 tubes for the Polaris A-3 missile (Crown Copyright (MOD-RN), London)
41(B) HMS *Superb* (S109) 'Swiftsure' class nuclear-powered fleet submarine, seen during contractor's trials in the Clyde estuary; June 1976 (Crown Copyright (MOD-RN), London)
42(T) HMS *Churchill* (S46) 'Valiant' class nuclear-powered fleet submarine off the Scottish coast; October 1970 (Crown Copyright (MOD-RN), London)
42(B) HMS *Orpheus* (S11) 'Oberon' class patrol submarine in the Clyde estuary; January 1978 (Crown Copyright (MOD-RN), London)
43) HMS *Hermes* (R12) anti-submarine carrier entering the Grand Harbour, Valletta; April 1977 (Crown Copyright (MOD-RN), London)
44(T) HMS *Tiger* (C20) 'Tiger' class helicopter cruiser enters Rotterdam harbour during a visit to Holland. HMS *Hermes* can be seen behind; September 1974 (Crown Copyright (MOD-RN), London)
44(B) HMS *Kent* (D12) 'County' class light cruiser off Gibraltar; 1978 (Crown Copyright (MOD-RN), London)
45) HMS *Newcastle* (D87) Type 42 guided-missile destroyer; March 1978 (Crown Copyright (MOD-RN), London)

46(T) HMS *Ariadne* (F72) 'Broad-beamed Leander' class frigate; August 1977 (Crown Copyright (MOD-RN), London)
46(B) HMS *Jupiter* (F60) 'Broad-beamed Leander' class frigate (Crown Copyright (MOD-RN), London)
47(T) HMS *Ashanti* (F117) 'Tribal' class frigate; 1973 (Crown Copyright (MOD-RN), London)
47(B) HMS *Salisbury* (F32) 'Salisbury' class frigate; December 1974 (Crown Copyright (MOD-RN), London)
48) HMS *Fearless* (L10) LPD assault ship showing her stern door lowered and landing craft operating from the dock between the two hulls; 1973 (Crown Copyright (MOD-RN), London)
49(T) HMS *Cuxton* (M1125) 'Ton' class coastal minesweeper leaves Faslane, Dunbartonshire, at the end of Clyde Week, July 1977 (Crown Copyright (MOD-RN), London)
49(B) HMS *Kingfisher* (P260) 'Bird' class large patrol craft leaving Rosyth; October 1975 (Crown Copyright (MOD-RN), London)
50(T) MM38 Exocet surface-to-surface missile being fired from HMS *Norfolk* (D21); 1974 (Crown Copyright (MOD-RN), London)
50(C) MM38 Exocet surface-to-surface missile being launched (Aérospatiale, Paris)
50(B) Sea Dart missiles on the Type 82 light cruiser HMS Bristol; May 1975 (Hawker Siddeley Dynamics, Herts.)
55(T) A Lightning F.2A of 19 Sqdn banking at low level (Crown Copyright (MOD-RAF), London)
55(B) A Vickers 1106 VC10 of the old Transport Command named 'George Thompson VC' in flight over England (Vickers Ltd., London)
56) A Canberra Mk 82 of the Venezuelan Air Force awaiting delivery at British Aerospace's Warton airfield (British Aerospace, Lancashire)
58(T) Harrier V/STOL strike aircraft demonstrating its vertical take-off capabilities (British Aerospace – Aircraft Group, Surrey)
58(B) Harrier V/STOL strike aircraft at rest (Crown Copyright (MOD-RAF), London)
59) Nimrod long-range maritime patrol and anti-submarine aircraft; 1969 (Crown Copyright (MOD-RAF), London)
60(T) Mock-up of the Hawker Siddeley Nimrod airborne early warning aircraft (British Aerospace, Kingston-upon-Thames)
60(B) An artist's impression of the Hawker Siddeley Sea Harrier in flight (Crown Copyright (MOD-RN), London)
61) Vulcan B.2 bomber of 101 Squadron based at RAF Waddington on a routine training flight; November 1976 (Crown Copyright (MOD-RAF), London)
62) Victor K.2 tanker about to refuel a second tanker; August 1977 (Crown Copyright (MOD-RAF), London)
63) Left-side view of US Air Force MAC317th Tactical Airlift Wing C–130 equipped with flares used as Infra-red Countermeasure (IRCM) taking off; 1976 (US Air Force)
64) RF-4E Phantom II recce aircraft of the former Imperial Iranian Air Force (McDonnell Douglas Corp., USA)
65) The first training prototype MRCA Tornado 03 takes off from the BAC Military Aircraft Division's Warton Aerodrome on its first flight; 5 August 1975 (British Aerospace Military Aircraft Division, Lancashire)
66) A SEPECAT Jaguar GR.1 single-seat tactical support aircraft (XW563) with a large drop tank dropping a bomb during a training exercise (Crown Copyright (MOD-RAF), London)
67) A broken-down Gazelle helicopter being lifted from a school playing-field in Northern Ireland by a Puma Helicopter; 25 October 1977 (Crown Copyright (MOD-Army), London)
68(T) CH-47C Chinook heavy helicopter of the former Imperial Iranian Army Aviation (Boeing Vertol, USA)
68(B) A Westland Scout helicopter of the British Army (Westland Helicopters Ltd., Yeovil)
69(T) A Westland Wessex Mark 5 helicopter of the Royal Navy (Westland Helicopters Ltd., Yeovil)
69(B) A Westland Whirlwind (Westland Helicopters Ltd., Yeovil)
70) Westland Sea King of the Royal Navy (Westland Helicopters Ltd., Yeovil)
71(T) A Westland Lynx in the livery of the Qatar Air Force (Westland Helicopters Ltd., Yeovil)
71(B) AS.12 air-to-surface missile, designed for use against fortified emplacements and for coastal defence, seen here fitted to a Westland Wasp helicopter of the Royal Navy (the naval version of this missile is the SS.12M) (Aérospatiale, Paris)
72(T) AS.30 air-to-surface missile on a French Air Force Mirage III (Aérospatiale, Paris)
72(B) Bloodhound medium/high altitude missile immediately after launch (British Aerospace Guided Weapons Division, Herts.)
73) Hawker Siddeley Red Top second-generation air-to-air guided missile mounted on the Lightning F.6 in the foreground (Hawker Siddeley Dynamics, Herts.)
74(T) Sky Flash medium-range all-weather air-to-air missile based on the Raytheon Sparrow – here seen fitted below an F-4 Phantom II test aircraft; 19 July 1976 (British Aerospace – Dynamics Group, Herts.)
74(B) Martel (Missile Anti-Radar & TELevision) air-to-surface precision tactical strike missile; the anti-radar variant (AS.37) is on the left with the TV version (AJ.168) on the right (Hawker Siddeley Dynamics, Herts.)
75(T) An RAF FGR.2 Phantom over Yorkshire armed with seven BL755 cluster bombs and four Sparrow and four Sidewinder air-to-air missiles; September 1975 (Crown Copyright, MOD REP(S)PG, London)
75(B) An AIM-7 Sparrow III air-to-air missile mounted on a modified UH-2C Seasprite helicopter; July 1972 (US Navy Official Photo)

Index